English in Focus

Series Editors: J. P. B. ALLEN and H. G. WIDDOWSON
Advisory Editor: RONALD MACKIN

ENGLISH IN FOCUS

English in Physical Science

J. P. B. ALLEN
H. G. WIDDOWSON

LONDON
OXFORD UNIVERSITY PRESS
1974

Oxford University Press, Ely House, London W.1

GLASGOW   NEW YORK   TORONTO   MELBOURNE   WELLINGTON
CAPE TOWN   IBADAN   NAIROBI   DAR ES SALAAM   LUSAKA   ADDIS ABABA
DELHI   BOMBAY   CALCUTTA   MADRAS   KARACHI   LAHORE   DACCA
KUALA LUMPUR   SINGAPORE   HONG KONG   TOKYO

ISBN 0 19 437510 2   (Student's Book)
0 19 437504 8   (Teacher's Edition)

© Oxford University Press 1974

PRINTED AND BOUND IN ENGLAND BY
HAZELL WATSON AND VINEY LTD
AYLESBURY, BUCKS

Contents

Introduction

The aim of this book is to develop a basic knowledge of how English is used for communication in the physical sciences. It is intended for students who already know how to handle the common English sentence patterns but who need to learn how these patterns are used in scientific writing to convey information and to develop logical arguments.

The exercises direct the student's attention to certain features of English which are specific to scientific writing. The aim is to provide the student with a strategy for reading more difficult scientific texts and to prepare him for making effective use of English in his own writing.

Although the emphasis is on English as a medium of expression in the physical sciences, the basic elements of the language have not been neglected. Pattern practice is provided, particularly in the grammar and paragraph writing sections of each unit, but this kind of work is always presented in relation to a scientific context and not simply as an exercise in making sentences for their own sake.

This book does not aim at teaching the subject-matter of science, and it does not aim at teaching grammatical structures and vocabulary as such. Its purpose is to show how language is used as a medium for the study of science, and so to give students a grounding in one particular set of communication skills in English.

Edinburgh   J. P. B. A.
October, 1973   H. G. W.

1 The Properties of Air

I READING AND COMPREHENSION

[1]The earth is surrounded by a layer of air. [2]This is between 150 and 200 km thick and is called the atmosphere.

[3]Air is invisible and therefore it cannot be seen. [4]But it occupies space and has weight in the same way visible substances do. [5]This fact is illustrated in Problems A and B.

Study the following statements carefully and write down whether they are true or not true according to the information expressed above. Then check your answers by referring to the solutions at the end of the passage.*

(a) A layer of air surrounds the earth.
(b) A layer of air is called an atmosphere.
(c) Air can be seen.
(d) Air is a visible substance.

[6]Air, then, takes up space and has weight. [7]The atmosphere, therefore, weighs down on the surface of the earth. [8]However, this weight cannot be felt pressing on us because air not only exerts a downward pressure, but it also exerts pressure upwards and sideways, and this pressure is balanced by the equal pressure which our blood exerts in all directions.

[9]In short, air exerts pressure in every direction.

(e) The atmosphere presses down on us.
(f) We can feel the weight of the atmosphere.
(g) Air only exerts pressure upwards and sideways.
(h) Air exerts an upward pressure.

*The following symbols are used in the solutions:
i.e.   that is to say
e.g. for example
=   equals/means the same as
≠   does not equal/mean the same as
∴   therefore

Solutions

(a)   The earth is surrounded by a layer of air. (1)
=   A layer of air surrounds the earth.

(b)   A layer of air = ANY layer of air.
A layer of air surrounds the earth. THIS layer of air is called the atmosphere. (1, 2)
i.e.   THE layer of air [which surrounds the earth] is called *the* atmosphere.
∴   It is NOT TRUE that a (= any) layer of air is called an atmosphere.

(c)   Air is invisible and therefore it cannot be seen. (3)
IS INVISIBLE means CANNOT BE SEEN
IS VISIBLE   means CAN BE SEEN
∴   Air CANNOT be seen.

(d)   it (i.e. air) occupies space and has weight in the same way visible substances do. (4)
∴   Air is a substance.
but Air is not a VISIBLE substance.
i.e. Air is an INVISIBLE substance.

(e)   The atmosphere ... weighs down on the surface of the earth. (7)
this weight cannot be felt pressing on us. (8)
∴   This weight presses down on us.
This weight = the weight of the atmosphere
∴   *The atmosphere presses down on us.*

(f)   The weight cannot BE FELT. (8)
=   We cannot FEEL the weight.
The weight of the atmosphere cannot be felt. (7)
i.e.   We CANNOT feel the weight of the atmosphere.

(g)   air *not only* exerts a downward pressure, *but* it *also* exerts pressure upwards and sideways. (8)
=   Air *not only* exerts pressure upwards and sideways, *but* it *also* exerts a downward pressure.
exerts a downward pressure = exerts a pressure downwards
∴   It is NOT TRUE that air only exerts pressure upwards and sideways.

(h)   Air exerts a pressure upwards.
=   *Air exerts an upward pressure.*

EXERCISE A *Contextual reference*

1. In sentence 2, *this* refers to:
   (a) The earth
   (b) The layer of air
2. In sentence 5, *this fact* refers to:
   (a) The fact that air is invisible and occupies space.
   (b) The fact that air is invisible and therefore cannot be seen.
   (c) The fact that air occupies space and has weight.
3. In sentence 8, *this weight* refers to:
   (a) The weight of the atmosphere.
   (b) The weight of the earth.
4. In sentence 8, *it* refers to:
   (a) The atmosphere
   (b) The earth
   (c) Air
5. In sentence 8, *this pressure* refers to:
   (a) The downward pressure of air.
   (b) The pressure which air exerts in every direction.
   (c) The pressure which air exerts upwards and sideways.

EXERCISE B *Rephrasing*

Rewrite the following sentences replacing the words printed in italics with expressions from the text which have the same meaning.

EXAMPLE
The layer of air which surrounds the earth is between 150 and 200 km thick.
The atmosphere is between 150 and 200 km thick.

1. Air *weighs down* on the surface of the earth.
2. Air exerts pressure *upwards, downwards and sideways.*
3. Air *cannot be seen* but occupies space in the same way as do *substances which can be seen.*
4. Air *takes up* space and has weight.
5. The fact that air occupies space *is shown* in Problems A and B.

EXERCISE C *Relationships between statements*

Place the following expressions in the sentences indicated. Replace and re-order the words in the sentences where necessary.

EXAMPLE
   since (3)
   Air is invisible and *therefore* it cannot be seen. (3)
= *Since* air is invisible, it cannot be seen.

   (a) consequently (3)
   (b) however (4)
   (c) in short (6)
   (d) it follows that (7)
   (e) nevertheless (8)
   (f) then (9)

EXERCISE D *Statements based on diagrams*

1. Draw the following diagram and complete it, by referring to the reading passage.

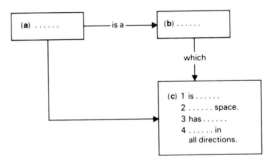

2. Use your completed diagram to write out as many sentences as you can as follows:
   (a) → (b) → (c)
   (a) → (c)
3. Use all the information in your completed diagram to write a *definition* of air in one sentence.

EXERCISE E *The writing of definitions*

Use the expressions in columns (b) and (c) in the following table to write appropriate definitions for the items in column (a).

EXAMPLE

   Hydrogen *is a* gas *which* is less dense than air.

a	b	c
lead		measures atmospheric pressure
propane		is less dense than air
a barometer	gas	burns at a high temperature
water	metal	measures electric current
hydrogen	liquid	is prepared by electrolysis
an ammeter	instrument	is used in thermometers
alcohol		contains hydrogen
aluminium		has a high relative density

II PROBLEMS
THE DESCRIPTION OF SIMPLE EXPERIMENTS

A. (1) Take a large plastic water can.
Make a hole in the cap.
Glue the valve from an old bicycle tyre into it.
Put the cap back on the can.
Weigh the can on a pair of balances.
Pump extra air into the can.
Weigh it again.
(2) The can weighs more after the extra air has been pumped into it than it did before.
(3) This shows that . . . (quote from the text)
Indicate the correct order of the following diagrams:

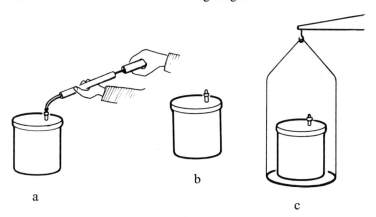

a

b

c

B. (1) Take a large glass container and half fill it with water.
Place a cork on the surface of the water.

Take a glass and lower it, mouth downward, over the cork and push it below the surface of the water.

(2) The air in the glass pushes the part of the surface which is under the glass below the surface of the surrounding water.

(3) This shows that . . . (quote from the text)

Draw a diagram of the result of this experiment (i.e. of (2)).

C. (1) Fill a glass to the brim with water.

Place a piece of cardboard over it.

Hold the cardboard against the glass and turn the glass upside down.

Take your hand away from the cardboard.

(2) The cardboard remains against the glass and the water remains in the glass.

(3) This shows that . . . (quote from the text)

Draw a diagram of the result of this experiment (i.e. of (2)).

D. Give a written version of the experiment illustrated below by using the notes provided.

Use Problems A–C as a guide and divide your version into three parts as shown:

(1) DIRECTIONS

Take large container—fill with water—take a glass—place in water—when the glass is full—hold the glass—mouth of the glass—surface of the water

(2) STATEMENT OF RESULT

The water—in the glass

(3) CONCLUSION

This shows—air—pressure—surface of the water

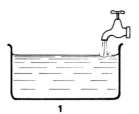
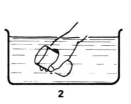

1   2   3

III GRAMMAR
EXERCISE A *Conditional sentences*

Look at the following sentence:

If   [**A** hot water is poured on to ice]   [**B** the ice will melt]

If [**A**] states when [**B**] is true.

Write ten sentences with a pattern if [**A**] [**B**]. Put each sentence from column **A** with a sentence from column **B** so that the complete sentence makes sense.

[A]	[B]
1. the mercury (II) oxide is heated	1. the charge which has the same sign as the inducing charge disappears
2. a layer of methylated spirit is floated on the surface of some water	2. fumes of nitrogen dioxide are driven out
3. a straight stick is inserted obliquely into water	3. the water is gradually pushed out by a colourless gas
4. we examine the works of a clock	4. it will be found to contain soil and fragments of plant material
5. one side of a block is rougher than the other sides	5. a uniform mixture of water and spirit will result
6. a bone is pulled into one position	6. it will appear to be bent at the surface of the water
7. the conductor is touched while the charged body is still near it	7. the nitrous acid is oxidized into nitric acid
8. an earthworm is opened	8. a second muscle is needed to pull it back into the first position
9. the solution is exposed to air for some time	9. friction is increased when the block rests on that surface
10. we heat some copper (II) nitrate in a dry tube	10. we will find that separate trains of wheels drive the hour hand and the minute hand

EXERCISE B *Sentences with* although *and* but

Note the following patterns:

    1. *although* [A] [B]   2. [A] *but* [B]

1. *Although* [air is invisible] [it is a substance which fills up space.]
2. [Air is invisible] *but* [it is a substance which fills up space.]

1. *Although* [lead is a base metal] [it has many important uses.]
2. [Lead is a base metal] *but* [it has many important uses.]

Write ten pairs of sentences, using (a) *although* (b) *but*. Put each sentence from column A with a sentence from column B so that the complete sentence makes sense.

[A]	[B]
1. the oil deposits are not very extensive	1. it burns if surrounded with an atmosphere of oxygen
2. light is a catalyst in this experiment	2. the efficiency of the engine was not seriously affected
3. man has affinities with the beasts	3. in larger animals this process would be too slow
4. there was a small leakage of steam	4. it frequently has to be purified
5. the direct measurement of the velocity of sound is not an easy experiment	5. they are still worth exploring
6. the majority of our engineering products are made of iron and steel	6. the problem can be attacked indirectly
7. ammonia will not catch fire in the air	7. heat rapidly causes the acid to distil over
8. water is never manufactured	8. he is unique in many intellectual and moral capacities
9. nothing happens when the retort is cold	9. other non-ferrous metals are sometimes used
10. in simple single-celled animals oxygen is directly absorbed	10. the reaction will take place slowly in the dark

IV   PARAGRAPH WRITING
STAGE 1 *Sentence building*

Join each of the groups of words below into one sentence, using the additional material at the beginning of each group. Omit words in italics. Number your sentences and begin each one with a capital letter.

EXAMPLE
1 THAT

we can show *this* air has weight	→ we can show . . . air has weight	→ We can show that air has weight.

2 THAT/RUSHING

| you know *this* air *rushes* along in the form of wind *air* can exert a large force on your body | → you know . . . air . . . along in the form of wind . . . can exert a large force on your body | → You know that air rushing along in the form of wind can exert a large force on your body. |

3 ALTHOUGH/IT/WHICH

air is invisible	→ air is invisible	→ Although air is invis-
air is a substance	... is a substance	ible it is a substance
air fills up space	... fills up space	which fills up space.

Now do these in the same way:

4 SO MUCH/THAT/TOTAL WEIGHT OF THE/SURROUNDING/
   AMOUNTS TO
there is *a lot of* air
the atmosphere *surrounds* the earth
the atmosphere weighs many million million tonnes
5 LITTLE MORE THAN
a cubic metre of air weighs *about* 1·2 kg
6 IF YOU/THAT/ITS
wave a large sheet of cardboard about
you will find *this*
the air resists *the* movement *of the cardboard*
7 SLIGHTLY HEAVIER/THAN IT WAS/WHEN/IT
the inner tube is *heavy*
there was no air in *the inner tube*
8 ,/IT/,/AND/IT
take a deflated inner tube from a bicycle tyre
weigh *the inner tube* on a pair of balances
inflate the inner tube
weigh *the inner tube* again

STAGE 2 *Paragraph building*

Rewrite the eight sentences in a logical order to make a paragraph. Before
you write the paragraph, make the following changes:

write 'by means of the following experiment' at the end of sentence 1
join sentence 2 and sentence 6 with 'and'
join sentence 5 and sentence 4 with 'but'.

When you have written your paragraph, re-read it and make sure that the
sentences are presented in a logical order. Give the paragraph a suitable
title. Compare your paragraph with the relevant paragraph in the Free
Reading passage on p. 10. Make any changes that you think are necessary,
but remember that sentences can often be arranged in more than one way.

STAGE 3 *Paragraph reconstruction*

Read through the paragraph again. Make sure you know all the words,
using a dictionary if necessary. Without referring to your previous work
rewrite the paragraph. Here are some notes to help you.

air – invisible – substance – space
air – wind – force – body
wave – cardboard – air – resist – movement
show – air – weight – experiment
inner tube – bicycle tyre
weigh – balances
inflate – inner tube
weigh
inner tube – heavier – no air in it
cubic metre – air – weighs – 1·2 kg
so much air – total weight – atmosphere – earth – tonnes

V FREE READING

Read the following passage in your own time. Try to find additional examples of the points you have studied in this Unit.

Although air is invisible it is a substance which fills up space. You know that air rushing along in the form of wind can exert a large force on your body, and if you wave a large sheet of cardboard about you will find that the air resists its movement. We can show that air has weight by means of the following experiment. Take a deflated inner tube from a bicycle tyre, weigh it on a pair of balances, inflate the inner tube and weigh it again. The inner tube is slightly heavier than it was when there was no air in it. A cubic metre of air weighs little more than 1·2 kg, but there is so much air that the total weight of the atmosphere surrounding the earth amounts to many million million tonnes.

Although the atmosphere exerts a very great pressure, we do not feel this pressure weighing down on us. This is because air does not only exert pressure in one direction. There is blood inside our bodies which exerts the same pressure as the air outside. We can show the pressure which is exerted by the atmosphere by means of the following experiment. Take a tin can which has a screw top and put a little water in it. Place the can on a stove and heat it until the water boils and steam comes out of the open top. The steam drives some of the air out of the can. Now remove the can from the stove and screw the cap on the top. Allow the can to cool and see what happens. When the can is hot, the pressure which is exerted by the steam and air inside the can is the same as the air pressure outside the can. But as the can cools down the steam inside condenses and the air and water vapour that remain exert less pressure than the air outside. This outside pressure will be enough to make the can collapse.

2 Acids

I READING AND COMPREHENSION

[1]An acid is a compound containing hydrogen which can be replaced, directly or indirectly, by a metal. [2]Its solution in water turns blue litmus red.

[3]Acids can be classified into two groups. [4]Acids which always contain the element carbon are called organic acids and they often come from growing things, like fruit. [5]Citric acid, which is found in lemons and oranges and other citrus fruits, and acetic acid, which is found in vinegar, are organic acids. [6]Acids which do not contain the element carbon are known as inorganic acids. [7]They are usually prepared from non-living matter. [8]Inorganic acids consist only of hydrogen and an acid radical. [9]Hydrochloric acid consists of hydrogen and the chloride radical, and sulphuric acid consists of hydrogen and the sulphate radical. [10]They are inorganic acids.

(a) All acids contain hydrogen.
(b) Inorganic acids contain the chloride radical.
(c) Organic acids always come from growing things.
(d) Lemons and oranges are not citrus fruits.

[11]The hydrogen in an acid is replaceable by a metal. [12]Acids can be divided into classes according to the number of atoms in each molecule which a metal can replace. [13]Those which have only one replaceable hydrogen atom in each molecule are known as monobasic acids. [14]Other acids may contain either two or three such replaceable hydrogen atoms in each molecule and these are known as dibasic and tribasic acids respectively. [15]All the atoms of hydrogen in the molecules of inorganic acids are replaceable by a metal. [16]Sulphuric acid is an inorganic acid which is dibasic. [17]Hydrochloric acid is an example of an inorganic acid which is monobasic. [18]Orthophosphoric acid, whose molecules contain three atoms of hydrogen, is tribasic. [19]Acetic acid molecules each contain four hydrogen atoms but only one of these can be replaced by a metal. [20]Acetic acid is monobasic.

(e) A molecule of hydrochloric acid contains one atom of hydrogen.
(f) Inorganic acids are monobasic.
(g) Hydrochloric acid is the only monobasic acid.
(h) A molecule of sulphuric acid contains three atoms of hydrogen.
(i) Orthophosphoric acid is an inorganic acid.

Solutions

(a) An acid is a compound containing hydrogen which can be replaced by a metal. (1)
∴ An acid contains hydrogen.
= *All acids contain hydrogen.*

(b) Sulphuric and hydrochloric acids are inorganic acids. (9, 10)
Inorganic acids consist only of hydrogen and an acid radical. (8)
i.e. Inorganic acids contain AN acid radical.
Hydrochloric acid consists of hydrogen and the chloride radical, and sulphuric acid consists of hydrogen and the sulphate radical. (9)
i.e. HYDROCHLORIC acid contains the CHLORIDE radical.
SULPHURIC acid contains the SULPHATE radical.
∴ It is NOT TRUE that all inorganic acids contain the chloride radical.

(c) Organic acids OFTEN (not always) come from growing things. (4)
i.e. Organic acids DO NOT ALWAYS come from growing things.

(d) lemons and oranges and OTHER CITRUS FRUITS (5)
i.e. Lemons and oranges ARE citrus fruits.

(e) Hydrochloric acid is an example of an inorganic acid which is monobasic. (17)
i.e. Hydrochloric acid is BOTH inorganic and monobasic.
Acids which have only one replaceable hydrogen atom in each molecule are known as monobasic acids. (13)
i.e. Monobasic acids have ONLY ONE REPLACEABLE hydrogen atom in each molecule.
but ALL the atoms of hydrogen in the molecules of inorganic acids are replaceable by a metal. (15)
∴ Hydrochloric acid has ONLY ONE hydrogen atom in each molecule.
= *A molecule of hydrochloric acid contains one atom of hydrogen.*

(f) Inorganic acids are monobasic.
= ALL inorganic acids are monobasic.
but Sulphuric acid is an inorganic acid which is also a dibasic acid. (16)
∴ It is NOT TRUE that inorganic acids (= all inorganic acids) are monobasic.

(g) Hydrochloric acid is AN EXAMPLE of an inorganic acid which is mono-basic. (17)

i.e. There are other monobasic acids.

∴ It is NOT TRUE that hydrochloric acid is the only monobasic acid.

(h) Other acids may contain either two or three replaceable hydrogen atoms in each molecule and these are known as dibasic and tribasic acids respectively. (14)

i.e. An acid which contains two replaceable atoms of hydrogen in each molecule is known as a dibasic acid.

An acid which contains three replaceable atoms of hydrogen in each molecule is known as a tribasic acid.

Sulphuric acid is a dibasic acid. (16)

∴ A molecule of sulphuric acid contains TWO atoms of hydrogen.

(i) An acid which contains three replaceable atoms of hydrogen in each molecule is known as a tribasic acid. (14)

Orthophosphoric acid, whose molecules contain three atoms of hydro-gen, is tribasic. (18)

= Orthophosphoric acid contains three atoms of hydrogen in each molecule AND it is tribasic.

i.e. ALL the atoms of hydrogen are replaceable.

ALL the atoms of hydrogen in the molecules of inorganic acids are replaceable by a metal. (15)

∴ *Orthophosphoric acid is an inorganic acid.*

EXERCISE A *Contextual reference*

1. In sentence 2, *its* refers to:
   (a) Acid
   (b) Hydrogen
   (c) Metal
2. In sentence 4, *they* refers to:
   (a) Acids
   (b) Organic acids
3. In sentence 10, *They* refers to:
   (a) Hydrogen and the chloride radical
   (b) Hydrogen and the sulphate radical
   (c) Hydrochloric acid and sulphuric acid
4. In sentence 13, *Those* refers to:
   (a) Classes
   (b) Acids
   (c) Atoms
5. In sentence 19, *these* refers to:
   (a) Acetic acid molecules
   (b) The four hydrogen atoms

EXERCISE B *Rephrasing*

Rewrite the following sentences replacing the words printed in italics with expressions from the text which have the same meaning. (Refer to Exercise B in Unit 1.)

1. All the *atoms of hydrogen* in the molecules of inorganic acids *are replaceable* by a metal.
2. Acids which do not contain the element carbon are *known as* inorganic acids.
3. Acids can be *divided into classes* according to the number of atoms in each molecule which *a metal can replace.*
4. Sulphuric acid *has two replaceable hydrogen atoms in each molecule.*
5. Orthophosphoric acid *contains* three atoms of hydrogen in each molecule.
6. Orthophosphoric acid, *whose molecules contain three atoms of hydrogen,* is tribasic.

EXERCISE C *Relationships between statements*

Place the following expressions in the sentences indicated. Replace and re-order the words in the sentence where necessary. (Refer to Exercise C in Unit 1.)

(a) can be defined as (1)   (e) however (15)
(b) are classified as (5)   (f) whereas (16+17)
(c) for example (9)   (g) although (19)
(d) therefore (10)   (h) therefore (20)

EXERCISE D *Statements based on diagrams: definitions*

Draw the following diagram and complete it by reference to the reading passage. Then use it to write out:

1. *definitions* of the different kinds of acid mentioned in the text as follows:
(a) → (b) → (c)

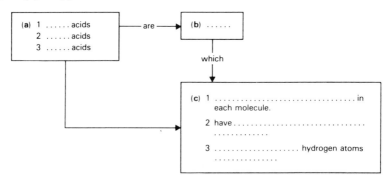

EXAMPLE
   Monobasic acids are acids which have one replaceable hydrogen atom in each molecule.

2. *generalizations* about the different acids mentioned in the text as follows:
(a) → (c)

EXAMPLE

Monobasic acids have one replaceable hydrogen atom in each molecule.

Now do the same with this diagram.

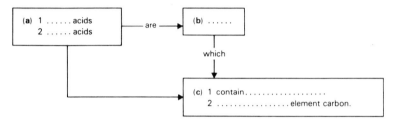

EXERCISE E *Statements based on diagrams: classifications*

1. Draw the following diagram and complete it by reference to the text, giving examples of the different classes of acid.

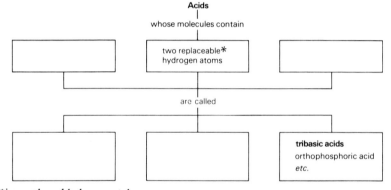

*i.e. replaceable by a metal

Use your completed diagram to make statements of the form:
Acids whose molecules contain . . . replaceable hydrogen atoms are called
. . . acids. . . . acid, for example, is a . . . acid.
2. Draw the following table and complete it by reference to the text. Give examples of the two classes of acid other than those mentioned in the reading passage.

Acids

+ carbon

acetic

Use your completed table to make statements of the form:
Acids which . . . carbon are called . . . acids.   . . . acid, for example, is an
. . . acid.

II PROBLEMS
THE CLASSIFICATION OF INFORMATION

A. Draw the table and arrange the following information in it.
1. *Acids:* hydrochloric, nitric, carbonic, sulphuric
2. *Acid radicals:* nitrate, carbonate, chloride, sulphate
3. *Molecular composition:**

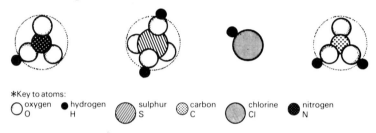

*Key to atoms:
oxygen   hydrogen   sulphur   carbon   chlorine   nitrogen
O   H   S   C   Cl   N

4. *Formulae:* HCl, H_2SO_4, H_2CO_3, HNO_3

1 Acid	2 Acid radical	3 Molecular composition	4 Formula	5 Monobasic/ dibasic

B. Use your table to write out:
(i) definitions of each of the four acids using the following framework:
. . . acid is a . . . acid whose molecules consist of . . . atom . . . and . . .
radical.
(ii) descriptions of each of the four radicals using the following framework:
The . . . radical consists of . . . .

III GRAMMAR
EXERCISE A *The forms of definitions*

Refer to Section I, Exercises D and E in Unit 1, and to Section I, Exercise D, in this Unit.

Definitions in scientific uses of English often take one of the following forms:

I

[A] *is/are, may be defined as* [B] *which* [C]

EXAMPLE

[A. A thermometer] *is* [B. an instrument] *which* [C. is used for measuring temperatures.]

A thermometer *is* an instrument *which* is used for measuring temperatures.

II

[B] *which* [C] *is/are called, is/are known as* [A]

EXAMPLE

[B. An instrument] *which* [C. is used for measuring temperatures] *is called* [A. a thermometer.]

An instrument *which* is used for measuring temperatures *is called* a thermometer.

Expand the following into full definitions. Write each sentence four times, using each of the patterns illustrated above.

1. metamorphosis/the physical transformation/is undergone by various animals during development after the embryonic stage
2. metals/the class of chemical elements/are characterized by ductility, malleability, lustre and conductivity
3. metaproteins/the group of substances/are produced by the action of acids or alkalis on proteins
4. latent heat/heat/is taken in or given out without change of temperature
5. a spectrum/the band of colours/can be formed by dispersing the light in a beam of mixed colours
6. an electromagnet/a soft iron core/temporarily becomes a magnet when an electric current flows through a coil of wire surrounding it
7. a supersaturated solution/a solution/contains rather more solute than is required to saturate it
8. a chloride ion/an atom of chlorine/has gained an electron and so become negatively charged

EXERCISE B *The impersonal passive*

The *impersonal passive* is very common in scientific writing. Examine the following active and passive sentences, and note that passive sentences contain some form of the verb 'to be' together with a past participle:

Active	Passive
we heat the mixture	the mixture is heated
we heated the mixture	the mixture was heated
we may heat the mixture	the mixture may be heated
we have heated the mixture	the mixture has been heated
the nitrogen monoxide extinguishes the glowing splint	the glowing splint is extinguished (by the nitrogen monoxide)

Note that the words in brackets are optional, and are often omitted in scientific writing.

Write down the passive version of all the following active sentences. Then join together the passive sentences you have written, following the clues provided.

EXAMPLE

Active: we examine the mixture under a microscope
Passive: the mixture *is examined* under a microscope
Active: we can see separate particles of iron and sulphur
Passive: separate particles of iron and sulphur *can be seen*

When the mixture *is examined* under a microscope, separate particles of iron and sulphur *can be seen*.

1. *Active:* we may show the expansion of a gas
   Passive: the expansion of a gas . . . .
   Active: we heat the gas
   Passive: the gas . . . . . .
   Active: we demonstrate an apparatus in Diagram 41
   Passive: an apparatus . . . . . . in Diagram 41

   The expansion of a gas when it . . . . . . may . . . . . . by the apparatus . . . in Diagram 41.

2. *Active:* we mentioned earlier that . . .
   Passive: it . . . . . . earlier that . . .
   Active: we can change a solid into a liquid by heating
   Passive: a solid . . . . into a liquid by heating
   Active: we can bring about the reverse change by cooling
   Passive: the reverse change . . . . about by cooling

   It . . . . . . earlier that a solid . . . . into a liquid by heating and that the reverse change . . . . about by cooling.

3. *Active:* we will find that . . .
   Passive: it . . . . that . . .

Active: we may refer to this statement as the law of levers
Passive: this statement . . . . to as the law of levers

. . . will . . . . . . that in every case effort ✕ effort arm = load ✕ load arm, and this statement . . . . to as the law of levers.

4. *Active:* we boil a little water in a tin can
Passive: a little water . . . . . . in a tin can
Active: steam fills the can
Passive: the can . . . . . . with steam
Active: we remove the can from the flame
Passive: the can . . . . . . from the flame
Active: we screw the top on the can
Passive: the top . . . . . . on the can
Active: we hold the can under a stream of cold water
Passive: the can . . . . . . under a stream of cold water

A little water . . . . . . in a tin can until the can . . . . . . with steam. The can . . . then . . . from the flame and the tap . . . . Then the can . . .
. . . under a stream of cold water from a tap.

5. *Active:* we carry out the heating of limestone on a large scale
Passive: the heating of limestone . . . . . . out on a large scale
Active: we use the name quicklime for calcium oxide
Passive: the name quicklime . . . . . . for calcium oxide
Active: we produce calcium oxide
Passive: calcium oxide . . . . . .

The heating of limestone . . . . . . out on a large scale in the manufacture of quicklime, which is the name commonly . . . for calcium oxide . . . .

6. *Active:* we must not allow water to come into contact with sodium
Passive: water . . . not . . . . . . to come into contact with sodium
Active: we keep the metal in a liquid such as naphtha
Passive: the metal . . . . . . in a liquid such as naphtha
Active: we should place the metal on a dry surface to cut it
Passive: the metal . . . . on a dry surface to . . . cut
Active: we should never touch the metal with our fingers
Passive: the metal . . . never . . . . . . with the fingers

Water . . . not . . . . . . to come into contact with large pieces of sodium. The metal . . . . . . in a liquid such as naphtha to protect it from water and . . . . on a dry surface to . . . . . . , and it . . . never . . . . . . with the fingers.

7. *Active:* we have described the movements
Passive: the movements . . . .
Active: the brain usually controls the movements
Passive: the movements . . . usually . . . by the brain

The movements which . . . . are usually . . . . . . the brain through the nervous system

8. *Active:* we form some salts from hydrochloric acid
   Passive: some salts . . . . . . from hydrochloric acid
   Active: we call these salts chlorides
   Passive: these salts . . . . . . chlorides

   All salts . . . from hydrochloric acid . . . . . . chlorides; all . . . from sulphuric acid . . . . . . sulphates; all . . . from nitric acid . . . . . . nitrates.

IV PARAGRAPH WRITING
STAGE 1 *Sentence building*

Join each of the eleven groups of words below into one sentence, using the additional material at the beginning of each group. Omit words in italics. Number your sentences and begin each one with a capital letter.

1 TURN/RED/AND/IT/,/GIVING
   an acid will *affect* litmus
   an acid will react with washing soda
   it will give off carbon dioxide

2 AND
   the metal disappears
   hydrogen is liberated

3 SPECIAL/,/,/AND/WHICH/TURN/BLUE
   a class of bases *is* called alkalis
   they will dissolve in water
   they will form solutions
   they will *affect* red litmus

4 OF HYDROGEN/WHICH/AND/WHEN
   an acid is a compound
   it will attack some metals
   it will liberate hydrogen
   magnesium is dissolved in it

5 WHICH/AND WHICH/OILY AND GREASY/,/AND FOR THIS REASON/
   FREQUENTLY
   alkalis form solutions
   they feel soapy
   they will dissolve substances
   they are used for cleaning

6 HAVE A BURNING EFFECT ON/LIKE/,/,/AND
acids *burn* substances
wood paper cloth human skin

7 INTO/A NUMBER OF DIFFERENT/,/OF WHICH
compounds can be divided
these are various classes *of compounds*
the most important *classes* are acids, bases and salts

8 MAY THUS/AS/WHEN/TAKES THE PLACE OF/IN AN ACID
we describe a salt
a salt is a substance
it is formed *in the following way*
a metal *replaces* hydrogen

9 ALWAYS/ONE OF THE PRODUCTS/WHEN/WITH A BASE,/OR/
BY AN ACID
a salt is *a product*
an acid is neutralized
a metal is dissolved

10 A CLASS OF SUBSTANCES/CONSISTING MAINLY OF/AND
HYDROXIDES/,/WHICH/IF/AND/IN THE PROCESS
bases are *substances*
the class contains oxides of metals
they will neutralize acids
they must be used in proper quantities
they form salt-like substances

11 IMPORTANT/OF COMPOUNDS
a third class consists of salts

STAGE 2 *Paragraph building*

Rewrite the eleven sentences in a logical order to make a paragraph. Before you write the paragraph, add the following material:

write 'in the latter case' at the beginning of sentence 2
write 'a further characteristic of acids is that they' at the beginning of sentence 6.

When you have written your paragraph, re-read it and make sure that the sentences are presented in a logical order. Give the paragraph a suitable title. Compare your paragraph with the relevant paragraph in the Free Reading passage. Make any changes that you think are necessary, but remember that sentences can often be arranged in more than one way.

STAGE 3 *Paragraph reconstruction*

Read through the paragraph again. Make sure you know all the words, using a dictionary if necessary. Without referring to your previous work rewrite the paragraph. Here are some notes to help you.

compounds – divided – acids – bases – salts
acid – compound of hydrogen – attack metals – liberate hydrogen – magnesium dissolved
acid – litmus red – washing soda – carbon dioxide
burn substances – wood, paper, etc.
    bases – oxides, hydroxides – neutralize acids – salt-like substances
alkalis – dissolve in water – litmus blue
alkalis – solutions – soapy – dissolve oil, grease – cleaning
salt – product – acid neutralized – metal dissolved
metal disappears – hydrogen liberated
salt – substance – metal takes place of hydrogen

V   FREE READING

Read the following passage in your own time. Try to find additional examples of the points you have studied in this Unit.

Substances consist of small parts, or particles, which are known as molecules. Molecules are composed of atoms. Some substances, like salt and water, have molecules which can be analysed further into other substances. If a molecule of water is analysed, for example, it will be found to consist of two atoms of hydrogen and one atom of oxygen. Substances whose molecules are composed of atoms of other substances are known as compounds. Other substances have molecules which cannot be broken down into atoms of other substances, and these are called elements. Hydrogen and oxygen, for example, are elements. Thus if a molecule of oxygen is analysed it will be found to consist of only atoms of oxygen and not of any other substance. There are 92 natural elements. Some are metallic solids like copper, iron and lead; some are non-metallic solids like sulphur and carbon; and some are gases like oxygen, hydrogen and nitrogen.

Compounds can be divided into a number of different classes, the most important of which are acids, bases and salts. An acid is a compound of hydrogen which will attack some metals and liberate hydrogen when magnesium is dissolved in it. An acid will turn litmus red and it will react with washing soda, giving off carbon dioxide. A further characteristic of acids is that they have a burning effect on substances like wood, paper, cloth and human skin. Bases are a class of substances, consisting mainly of oxides and hydroxides of metals, which will neutralize acids if used in proper quantities and form salt-like substances in the process. A special class of bases, called alkalis, will dissolve in water and form solutions which turn red litmus blue. Alkalis form solutions which feel soapy and which will dissolve oily and greasy substances, and for this reason they are frequently used for cleaning. A third important class of compounds consists of salts. A salt is always one of the products when an acid is neutralized with a base or a metal is dissolved by an acid. In the latter case the metal disappears and hydrogen is liberated. We may thus describe a salt as a substance formed when a metal takes the place of hydrogen in an acid.

Let us consider an example of a process which illustrates the relationship between acids, bases and salts. If a solution of sodium hydroxide is poured into a beaker containing hydrochloric acid and red litmus, the litmus will turn blue. This shows that the acid has been neutralized and that sodium hydroxide is a base. As a result of the neutralization of the acid by the base, sodium chloride is formed and may be obtained as crystals by evaporation of the solution. Thus the result of adding the base sodium hydroxide to hydrochloric acid is to form a salt, sodium chloride. This substance forms as a result of the metal sodium replacing the hydrogen in the acid. We may express this by means of the following formula:

$$\underset{\text{BASE}}{2NaOH} + \underset{\text{ACID}}{HCl} = \underset{\text{SALT}}{NaCl} + \underset{\text{WATER}}{H_2O}$$

3 Matter and Volume

[1]Matter is the name given to everything which has weight and occupies space. [2]It may usually be detected by the senses of touch, sight or smell.

[3]Matter may exist in three states: solid, liquid and gas. [4]All substances, except those which decompose when heated, like wood, may be changed from one state into another. [5]A substance in the solid state may be changed into a liquid substance, and one in the liquid state may be changed into a gaseous substance. [6]Changes can take place in the reverse order as well: gases may be changed into liquids and liquids into solids. [7]A solid substance such as ice may be changed into the liquid state, or liquefied, to become water; and this may be changed into the gaseous state, or evaporated, to become steam. [8]Steam may also be converted into water and water into ice.

(a) Matter can usually be seen, smelt or touched.
(b) Matter can be seen, smelt and touched.
(c) All substances can be changed from one state into another.
(d) A liquid can be changed either into a gas or into a solid.

[9]All matter occupies space. [10]The space occupied by a quantity of matter is called its volume, and this is usually measured in units such as cubic metres or cubic centimetres. [11]Solids have a definite volume and shape, liquids have a definite volume but no shape; the latter take on the shape of the container in which they rest. [12]Gases have no definite volume and no shape.

[13]The volume of a piece of solid substance, or body, of regular shape, like a cube, a sphere or a cylinder, may be calculated by using mathematical formulae of the following kind:

Volume of cube $= \text{length} \times \text{breadth} \times \text{height}$
Volume of sphere $= \frac{4}{3}\pi \times (\text{radius})^3$
Volume of cylinder $= \pi \times (\text{radius})^2 \times \text{height}$

[14]The volumes of irregular bodies cannot be calculated by the use of formulae of this kind. [15]They may be measured by means of devices like displacement vessels and measuring jars.

(e) Volume is measured in cubic metres or cubic centimetres.
(f) Substances have a definite volume and shape.
(g) Gases have no volume.
(h) All bodies have a definite shape.
(i) A cylinder is a regular body.
(j) The volumes of all bodies can be calculated in the same way.

Solutions

(a) MAY = CAN
     may usually be detected by the senses of touch, sight or smell. (2)
=   can usually be touched, seen or smelt.
∴.   *Matter can usually be seen, smelt or touched.*

(b) touched, seen or smelt.
=   EITHER touched OR seen OR smelt.
i.e. Some matter can be seen but not touched (e.g. visible gases)
     Some matter can be smelt but not seen (e.g. some invisible gases) etc.
     Matter can be seen, smelt and touched.
=   ALL matter can be seen AND smelt AND touched.
∴.   It is NOT TRUE that matter can be seen, smelt and touched.

(c) All substances, EXCEPT THOSE WHICH DECOMPOSE WHEN HEATED, may be changed from one state into another. (4)
∴.   Some substances cannot (= may not) change from one state to another.
∴.   It is NOT TRUE that all substances can be changed from one state to another.

(d) A substance in the liquid state may be changed into a gaseous substance. (5)
i.e. A liquid can be changed into a gas.
     gases may be changed into liquids and liquids [may be changed] into solids. (6)
∴.   *A liquid can be changed* EITHER *into a gas* OR [*into*] *a solid.*

(e) Volume is USUALLY (not always) measured in units SUCH AS cubic metres or cubic centimetres (or others). (10)
     Volume is measured in cubic metres or cubic centimetres.
=   Volume is ALWAYS measured in cubic metres or cubic centimetres.
∴.   It is NOT TRUE that volume is (always) measured in cubic metres or cubic centimetres.

(f) SOLIDS have a definite volume and [a definite] shape. (11)
   Liquids and gases are also substances.
   Liquids have no shape (11) and gases have no definite volume and no shape. (12)
∴   Substances do not ALL have definite volume and shape.
∴   It is NOT TRUE that substances have a definite volume and shape.

(g) Gases have no DEFINITE volume. (12)
≠   Gases have no volume (at all).
   All matter occupies space. (9)
   Gases are matter. (3)
∴   Gases occupy space. = Gases have volume.
∴   It is NOT TRUE that gases have no volume.

(h) Solids have a definite shape. (11)
   A body is a piece of solid substance. (13)
i.e.   A body is a solid.
∴   A body has a definite shape.
=   *All bodies have a definite shape.*

(i) A cylinder is a piece of solid substance of regular shape. (13)
   a piece of solid substance of regular shape
=   a body of regular shape = a regular body.
∴   *A cylinder is a regular body.*

(j) The volumes of REGULAR BODIES are calculated by formulae of the kind given in (13).
   The volumes of IRREGULAR BODIES cannot be calculated by the use of formulae of this kind. (14)
∴   The volumes of all bodies CANNOT be calculated in the same way.

EXERCISE A *Contextual reference*

1. In sentence 2, *It* refers to:
    (a) Weight
    (b) Space
    (c) Matter
2. In sentence 5, *one* refers to:
    (a) A substance
    (b) A substance in the solid state
    (c) A liquid substance
3. In sentence 7, *this* refers to:
    (a) A solid substance
    (b) Water
    (c) Ice

4. In sentence 10, *this* refers to:
   (a) A quantity of matter
   (b) Its volume
5. In sentence 11, *the latter* refers to:
   (a) Solids
   (b) Liquids
   (c) A definite volume
6. In sentence 15, *They* refers to:
   (a) Irregular bodies
   (b) Formulae
   (c) The volumes of irregular bodies

EXERCISE B *Rephrasing*

Rewrite the following sentences replacing the words printed in italics with expressions from the text which have the same meaning.
1. *A substance in the solid state* may be changed into *a liquid substance.*
2. *Gases* may be changed into *liquids* and *liquids* may be changed into *solids.*
3. A solid may be *changed into the liquid state.*
4. A liquid may be *changed* into a gas.
5. The volumes of *bodies of regular shape*, like cubes, are calculated *by using* mathematical formulae.
6. The volumes of *irregular bodies* may be measured *by means of* measuring jars.
7. Water may be *changed into the gaseous state* to become steam.

EXERCISE C *Relationships between statements*

Place the following expressions in the sentences indicated. Replace and re-order the words in the sentences where necessary.
   (a) can be defined as (1)
   (b) thus (5)
   (c) also (6)
   (d) thus (6)
   (e) for example (7)
   (f) then (7)
   (g) then (9)
   (h) whereas (11)
   (i) however (14)

EXERCISE D *Statements based on diagrams: generalizations*

1. Draw the following diagram and complete it by referring to the reading passage.

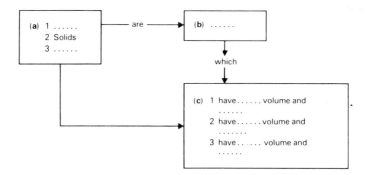

2. Use your completed diagram to:
   (i) Write *definitions*: (a) → (b) → (c)
   (ii) Write *generalizations*: (a) → (c)

EXAMPLES
   (i) Definition: Solids are substances which have a definite volume and a definite shape.
   (ii) Generalization: Solids have a definite volume and a definite shape.

3. The same definition may be expressed in more than one way. Refer to Section III, Exercise A, in Unit 2 and use the information in the diagram above to write out as many definitions as you can.
NOTE: Type I forms: (a) → (b) → (c)
        Type II forms: (b) → (c) → (a)
4. The same generalization may be expressed in more than one way.

EXAMPLE
        (a) Solids have a definite volume and a definite shape.
   =   (b) A solid has a definite volume and a definite shape.
   =   (c) All solids have a definite volume and a definite shape.

Express the generalizations you have written out in 2 above in different ways.

5. Consider the following statements:

   (a) All substances, except those which decompose when heated, can be changed from one state to another.
   (b) A solid substance can be changed into a liquid substance.

Statement (b) follows logically from statement (a). If (a) is true then (b) must also be true.
   Both statements are generalizations, but (a) is a higher level generalization than (b).
(i) Use the following diagram to write out as many lower level generalizations like statement (b) as you can.

EXAMPLE
A solid may be changed into a substance in the liquid state.
A substance in the solid state may be changed into a liquid.
A gaseous substance may be changed into a liquid substance.*

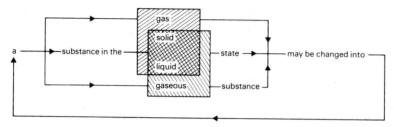

(ii) Express these generalizations in the different ways shown in 4 above.

EXERCISE E *Transforming definitions into generalizations*

Refer back to the definitions you have written out in Section I, Exercise E, Unit 1 and Section I, Exercise D, Unit 2, and change them into generalizations.

EXAMPLE (Exercise E, Unit 1)
Definition: A barometer is an instrument which measures atmospheric pressure.
(*or* Barometers are instruments which measure atmospheric pressure.)
Generalization: A barometer measures atmospheric pressure.
(*or* Barometers measure atmospheric pressure.)

EXAMPLE (Exercise D, Unit 2)
Definition: Monobasic acids are acids whose molecules contain one replaceable hydrogen atom.
(*or* A monobasic acid is an acid whose molecules contain one replaceable hydrogen atom.)
Generalization: Monobasic acids contain one replaceable hydrogen atom.
(*or* A monobasic acid contains one replaceable hydrogen atom.)
The molecules of a monobasic acid contain one replaceable hydrogen atom.
(*or* The molecules of monobasic acids contain one replaceable hydrogen atom.)
(*or* Molecules of monobasic acids contain one replaceable hydrogen atom.)
(*or* A molecule of a monobasic acid contains one replaceable hydrogen atom.)

* These generalizations are, of course, only true for substances which do not decompose when heated.

II PROBLEMS
INFORMATION TRANSFER

A. Draw the table below and arrange the following information in it.

1. *Regular bodies:* cube, cylinder, cone, sphere
2. *Shapes:*

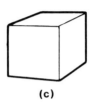

(a)   (b)   (c)   (d)

3. *Volumes:* l(ength) $\times$ b(readth) $\times$ h(eight), $\frac{4}{3}\pi \times r^3$,

$$\pi r^2 \times h, \qquad \pi r^2 \times \frac{h}{3} \qquad (\pi = 3 \cdot 14)$$

EXAMPLE

1 Body	2 Shape	3 Volume
cube		l x b x h

B. Make statements about the objects illustrated below by using the following terms:

cube	cubical
sphere	spherical
cone	conical
cylinder	cylindrical

← 8cm →   ← 20 cm →   12cm   14 cm

A   B   C   D

EXAMPLE

Object A is a cube.
Object A is in the shape of a cube.
Object A is cubical.
Object A is cubical in shape.
} Its volume is ... cm³,
or ... m³.

C. Read this description of an experiment.

The measurement of the volume of irregular solids

Water is poured into the displacement vessel until it overflows through the pipe into the measuring jar. The level of the water surface in the measuring jar is read, and then the solid is lowered into the vessel until it is completely covered by the water. Water is displaced and flows down the pipe into the measuring jar, and the level of the water surface in the measuring jar is read again. The volume of water displaced is equal to the volume of the body.

(i) Draw the diagram below and label it. Then draw a second diagram to illustrate the measurement of the volume of irregular solids described above.

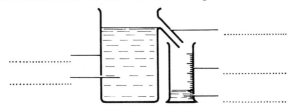

(ii) Change the description of measurement given above into a set of directions etc. for measuring the volume of irregular solids by using the following framework and by referring to the problems in Unit 1.

(1) DIRECTIONS

Take a displacement vessel and a measuring jar.

. . . .
. . . .
. . . .

(2) STATEMENT OF RESULT

Water is displaced and flows down the pipe into the measuring jar.

(1) DIRECTIONS

. . . .

(2) STATEMENT OF RESULT

The volume of water displaced is equal to the volume of the body.

III GRAMMAR

EXERCISE A *Combining sentences with an* -ing *clause*

Look at the following sentences:

(a) The light is deflected.
(b) The deflection depends on the angle of inclination.

These can be combined into one sentence:

(c) The light is deflected, the deflection depending on the angle of inclination.

Notice what changes are made:

The light is deflected. The deflection *depends* on the angle of inclination.

The light is deflected, the deflection *depending* on the angle of inclination.

Combine each of the following pairs of sentences into one sentence by using an -ing clause in the same way:

1. Two rods, of metal and wood respectively, are joined end to end in a straight line. The wooden end of the composite rod projects at right angles over the edge of the table.
2. If a belt or chain connects wheels of different diameters, the number of revolutions of these wheels will not be the same in a given time. The smaller wheels make the greater number of revolutions.
3. The periscope, which is the 'eye' of the submarine when submerged, can be raised above the surface of the water. The other end of it is in the control room.
4. When paraffin wax is melted in a boiling-tube and allowed to cool, the wax in contact with the sides of the tube solidifies first. The contraction of the bulk of the wax causes a crater to form on the surface.
5. In an arrangement of gear wheels two cog wheels are in direct contact. The teeth of one wheel engage with the teeth of the other.
6. In petrol engines the power is produced by the expansion of gases in a cylinder by heating. The fuel for combustion is a mixture of petrol vapour and air.
7. The process continues until the temperature is lowered sufficiently for liquid air to be produced. The liquid air is collected in a vacuum flask.
8. The hot gas passes into a condenser where it is cooled and condensed to liquid ammonia. The high pressure in the apparatus helps in this process.
9. Living creatures and plants give water vapour to the air in considerable quantities. A human being under normal conditions emits about 63 g of water vapour per hour.
10. There are four main types of cloud formation. Each is subdivided into several classes.
11. If an attempt is made to increase the pressure of a saturated vapour by compression some of the vapour condenses. The vapour pressure remains constant.
12. Heat and light energy are propagated by transverse waves. The commonest example of such waves is found in water.

EXERCISE B *Defining and non-defining relative clauses*

Look at the following sentences:

(a) Machines must be provided with a protective casing.
(b) Machines are dangerous.

If the noun phrase *machines* refers to the same thing in each sentence, we can combine the two sentences into one:

(c) Machines which are dangerous must be provided with a protective casing.

Notice what changes are made:

Machines ⌒ must be provided with a protective casing.
⌐machines are dangerous⌐
↓
Machines   which are dangerous must be provided with a protective casing.

Now compare the following sentences:

(d) The machine which is dangerous must be provided with a protective casing.
(e) The machine, which is dangerous, must be provided with a protective casing.

In sentence **(d)**, the clause *which is dangerous* tells us what kind of machine we are talking about. It is a *defining relative clause*.

In sentence **(e)**, the clause *, which is dangerous,* tells us something extra about the machine we are talking about. It is a *non-defining relative clause*. Note the use of commas.

Combine each of the following pairs of sentences into a single sentence. Make the second sentence into a relative clause and insert it into the first sentence at the place marked by dots. Note whether the relative clause is a defining one or a non-defining one.

EXAMPLE
  Zinc oxide is a white powder . . . . The powder becomes yellow when it is heated.
  Zinc oxide is a white powder which becomes yellow when it is heated. (defining)

1. Evaporate the solution and a white residue . . . will be obtained. The residue is not deliquescent.
2. Alkalis have the special property of forming solutions . . . . The solutions will dissolve oily and greasy substances.
3. The experiment illustrates the fact that there is something which might be described as 'electrical pressure', . . . 'Electrical pressure' decides the movement of electrical charges. (There are two relative clauses in this sentence. Underline them both in your notebook. Which clause is defining and which is non-defining?)
4. Conductors of this second class, . . . , are called electrolytes. They are decomposed when an electric current passes.
5. Much scientific information can be summarized in statements . . . . The statements are known as scientific laws.

6. The Daniell cell, . . ., is very similar to a simple cell. The Daniell cell was formerly much used by the Post Office.

7. The single conductor . . . will also be found to be positively charged. The conductor was touched before the ebonite rod was removed.

8. A sharp-smelling colourless gas will be given off, . . . The gas forms whitish fumes as it escapes into the air.

9. Hydrochloric acid solution, . . ., is used for cleaning sheets of iron before coating them with tin or zinc. Hydrochloric acid solution is often known commercially as spirits of salt.

10. The figure indicates one molecule of sulphuric acid . . ., but remember that there would be millions of such molecules in the solution. One molecule of sulphuric acid has not broken up.

11. The chemical changes . . . can be reversed by driving a current through it in the opposite direction to the current it gives out. The chemical changes take place in the cell when it is giving out current.

12. If hot saturated solutions of sodium nitrate and potassium chloride are mixed, sodium chloride, . . ., is precipitated and potassium nitrate can be obtained by filtering off the sodium chloride and cooling the filtrate. Sodium chloride is less soluble in hot water than the other substances present.

IV   PARAGRAPH WRITING
STAGE 1 *Sentence building*

Join each of the twelve groups of words below into one sentence, using the additional material at the beginning of each group. Omit words in italics. Number your sentences and begin each one with a capital letter.

1   THERE WILL BE NO CHANGE IN/AS/A GREATER DEPTH
the reading *will not change*
the stone is lowered
*the stone goes in*to *deeper water*

2   BY MEANS OF A THREAD/AND/GRADUALLY/CONTAINING
hang a stone from a spring balance
lower the stone into a vessel
the vessel contains water

3   THAT/APPARENT
we find *this*
the loss of weight is 3 g

4   THERE ARE/BUT IMPORTANT/APPLICATIONS OF
several simple *ways to apply* this principle *exist*

5 AS SOON AS/,/SHOWING THAT/EXERTS AN UPTHRUST/ON THE
STONE
the stone touches the water
the spring balance reading is reduced
the water *thrusts upwards*

6 IF/THEN/GRADUALLY/,/BALANCE
the stone is withdrawn from the water
the changes in the reading will be reversed

7 , SUCH AS A LARGE ROCK,/WHEN IT/,/BUT/AS SOON AS/IT
a heavy body can be raised easily
the body is under water
the body seems to be much heavier
the body comes out into the air

8 IF/AN IRREGULAR/MAY/AND/THEN/IT
we want to find the volume of *a* solid
we weigh the solid
the solid is hanging in air
we reweigh *the solid*
the solid is hanging in water

9 AND THEREFORE/,/WHICH
the water *is* displaced
the water has a mass of 3 g
the water has a volume of 3 cm^3
this must be the volume of the solid

10 THE APPARENT LOSS OF/WHEN
a body apparently loses weight
a body is placed in liquid
this may be demonstrated as follows

11 ACCOUNTED FOR/THE GREEK PHILOSOPHER/,/WHO/THAT/
THE APPARENT LOSS OF WEIGHT OF/WHEN IT
these facts were *explained* by Archimedes
he stated *this*
a body is immersed in a liquid
the apparent loss of weight is equal to the weight of liquid displaced

12 WILL CONTINUE TO GET/AS/MORE OF/,/UNTIL/COMPLETELY
the spring balance reading *gets* smaller
the stone enters the water
the stone is immersed

STAGE 2 *Paragraph building*

Rewrite the twelve sentences in a logical order to make a paragraph. Before
you write the paragraph, add the following material:

write 'suppose' at the beginning of sentence 3
write 'for example' at the beginning of sentence 8
write 'then' at the beginning of sentence 9.

When you have written your paragraph, re-read it and make sure that the sentences are presented in a logical order. Give the paragraph a suitable title. Compare your paragraph with the relevant paragraph in the Free Reading passage. Make any changes that you think are necessary, but remember that sentences can often be arranged in more than one way.

STAGE 3 *Paragraph reconstruction*

Read through the paragraph again. Make sure you know all the words, using a dictionary if necessary. Without referring to your previous work, rewrite the paragraph. Here are some notes to help you.

heavy body – raised easily – under water – much heavier – in the air
loss of weight – in liquid – demonstrated as follows
stone – spring balance – lower – water
touches water – reading reduced – upthrust on stone
reading – smaller – until completely immersed
no change – reading – greater depth
stone gradually withdrawn – reading reversed
Archimedes stated . . .
find the volume of an irregular solid
apparent loss of weight $= 3$ g
mass of water displaced $= 3$ g, volume of water displaced $= 3$ cm^3,
volume of solid $= 3$ cm^3

V   FREE READING

Read the following passage in your own time. Try to find additional examples of the points you have studied in this and other Units.

A heavy body, such as a large rock, can be raised easily when it is under water, but seems to be much heavier as soon as it comes out into the air. The apparent loss of weight when a body is placed in liquid may be demonstrated as follows. Hang a stone from a spring balance by means of a thread and gradually lower the stone into a vessel containing water. As soon as the stone touches the water the spring balance reading is reduced, showing that the water exerts an upthrust on the stone. The spring balance reading will continue to get smaller as more of the stone enters the water, until the stone is completely immersed. There will be no change in the reading as the stone is lowered to a greater depth. If the stone is then gradually withdrawn from the water, the changes in the balance reading will be reversed. These facts were accounted for by the Greek philosopher Archimedes, who stated that the apparent loss of weight of a body when it is immersed in a liquid is equal to the weight of liquid displaced. There are several simple but important applications of this principle. For example, if we want to find the volume of an irregular solid we may weigh the solid hanging in air and then reweigh it hanging in water. Suppose we find that the apparent loss of weight is 3 g. Then the water displaced has a mass of 3 g and therefore has a volume of 3 cm³, which must be the volume of the solid.

To find the relative density of a solid, first weigh a piece of the solid in air and then in water as described above. Let the two weights be W and w respectively. Relative density is equal to the weight of the solid divided by the weight of the same volume of water. However, by the principle of Archimedes the weight of the same volume of water is equal to the apparent loss of weight. Therefore the relative density of the solid is equal to the weight of the solid divided by the apparent loss in weight, i.e. : $\dfrac{W}{W-w}$.

Suppose now that we want to find the relative density of a liquid, say paraffin. Weigh a solid in air, then in water and finally in paraffin. Let these weights be W, w_1 and w_2 respectively. The relative density of paraffin is equal to the weight of a certain volume of paraffin divided by the weight of an equal volume of water. The volume in each case is that displaced by the solid. The weight of this volume of paraffin is equal to the apparent loss of weight of the solid in paraffin $= W-w_2$. Similarly, the weight of the same volume of water $= W-w_1$, therefore the relative density of paraffin $= \dfrac{W-w_2}{W-w_1}$.

When a heavy body such as a stone or a piece of iron is suspended on a string and totally immersed in water, there are three forces acting on it: the downward force due to the weight of the object (W), the upthrust (w) due to the displaced water, and the tension (T) of the supporting string. When the suspended object is in equilibrium, $W = T+w$. Suppose now we suspend a piece of wood on a string and lower the wood into water. The wood will float and the tension of the string will be reduced to zero, resulting in the equation $W = w$. In other words, when an object floats in a fluid, the weight of the object is equal to the weight of the fluid displaced. This statement is called the *law of flotation*. The law may be verified as follows. Take a test-tube and load it with just enough lead shot to enable the tube to float upright in water. Remove the tube from the water, wipe it dry and weigh it in order to find the total weight of the floating object. Find the weight of water displaced by the test-tube by using a graduated cylinder or a eureka can. It will be found that the weight of the object is equal to the weight of water displaced, thus verifying the law of flotation.

4 Force and Pressure

---

[1]A liquid presses on the sides and on the bottom of the container in which it rests. [2]It exerts a force both sideways and downwards. [3]The sides of a cardboard carton of milk will often curve outwards, and this is caused by the sideways force exerted by the milk. [4]Wooden barrels and water tanks are usually strengthened with metal bands: they are reinforced to resist the sideways force exerted by the liquid in these containers.

[5]A liquid also exerts a force upwards on any object which is placed in it. [6]If you push a rubber ball or a plastic boat under the surface of the water in a container, you will feel the upward force against the bottom of these objects.

[7]A liquid exerts a force in every direction.

(a)   The sides of a cardboard carton of milk curve outwards.
(b)   Wooden water tanks are usually strengthened with metal bands.
(c)   Wooden barrels are usually reinforced.
(d)   All liquids exert an upward force.
(e)   Water exerts a force in every direction.

[8]When a liquid presses against the container in which it rests, we say that it exerts a force. [9]Force, however, is not the same as pressure.

[10]A block of metal of mass 10 kg resting on a flat surface such as a table exerts a downward force of about 98 newtons. [11]The downward force exerted by an object is the same as its weight and we measure weight in force units called newtons. [12]But the object does not exert a pressure of 98 N. [13]The pressure which is exerted depends on the area of contact between the object and the table. [14]Pressure is measured by the force divided by the area of the surface on which it acts.

(f) Objects A and B exert the same downward force.

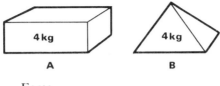

(g) Pressure $= \dfrac{\text{Force}}{\text{Area of contact}}$

[15]Let us suppose that the area of one of the surfaces of an oblong block of steel weighing 200 N is 200 cm² (0·02 m²). [16]If the object is placed on a table-top so that this surface is in contact with the surface of the table, the pressure between the object and the table will be 200N/200 cm², which is 10,000 N/m². [17]If the other surface of the object measures 100 cm² (0·01 m²), and if this makes contact with the table-top, the pressure between the object and the table will be 200 N/100 cm², which equals 20,000 N/m². [18]The force exerted by the object is the same in each case, but the pressure varies. [19]Less pressure is exerted when the area of contact is large, and more pressure is exerted when the area of contact is small.

[20]The pressure exerted by solid objects depends on the area of contact. [21]The pressure exerted by liquids, on the other hand, depends on depth. [22]The pressure at any point in a free-standing liquid is directly proportional to its depth below the surface. [23]If a point, A, is twice as far below the surface as another point, B, the pressure at A will be twice as great as the pressure at B.

(h) The pressure exerted by a solid object weighing 200 N is 10,000 N/m².
(i) Two objects of different weights may exert the same pressure.
(j) Pressure in liquids increases with depth.
(k) The pressure at point B is three times as great as the pressure at point A.

Solutions

(a) The sides of a cardboard carton of milk curve outwards.
=   The sides of a cardboard carton of milk ALWAYS curve outwards.
but The sides of a cardboard carton of milk will OFTEN (i.e. not always) curve outwards. (3)
∴   It is NOT TRUE that the sides of a cardboard carton of milk (always) curve outwards.

(b)   A N_1 N_2
       Wooden   barrels   and water tanks (4)
=   EITHER (i) $A+(N_1+N_2)$
i.e. Wooden (barrels and water tanks)
       OR (ii) $(A+N_1)+N_2$
i.e. (Wooden barrels) and water tanks
if (i) *Wooden water tanks are usually strengthened with metal bands.*

(c) reinforce = strengthen
∴   Wooden barrels are usually strengthened (with metal bands) (4)
=   *Wooden barrels are usually reinforced.*

(d) A liquid exerts a force in every direction. (7)
∴   A liquid exerts a force upwards.
=   A liquid exerts an upward force.
=   *All liquids exert an upward force.* (See Exercise D 4, Unit 3)

(e) A liquid exerts a force in every direction. (7)
       Water is a liquid.
∴   *Water exerts a force in every direction.*

(f) The downward force exerted by an object is the same as its weight.
       (11)
       Objects A and B have the same weight.
∴   *Objects A and B exert the same downward force.*

(g) $\dfrac{\text{Force}}{\text{Area of contact}}$
=   Force divided by the area of contact.
       area of contact = area of the surface on which the force acts (13, 14)
∴   Pressure is measured by the force divided by the area of the surface on
       which it acts. (14)
i.e. $Pressure = \dfrac{Force}{Area\ of\ contact}$

(h) The pressure exerted by a solid object weighing 200 N is 10,000 N/m².
=   The pressure exerted by a solid object weighing 200 N is ALWAYS
       10,000 N/m².
but The pressure exerted by a solid object depends on the area of contact. (20)
       The pressure exerted by a solid object weighing 200 N is 10,000 N/m²
       ONLY IF the area of contact is 0·02 m². (15, 16)
∴   It is NOT TRUE that the pressure exerted by an object weighing 200 N is
       (always) 10,000 N/m².

(i) The downward force exerted by an object is the same as its weight. (11) Pressure is measured by the force divided by the area of the surface on which it acts. (14)

∴ Two objects of different weights may exert the same pressure, although they do not exert the same force.

e.g. Object A exerts the same pressure as object B:

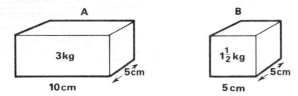

Two objects of different weights may exert the same pressure.

(j) If a point, A, is twice as far below the surface as another point, B, the pressure at A will be twice as great as the pressure at B. (23)

i.e. The pressure at A is greater than the pressure at B.

∴ *Pressure in liquids increases with depth.*

(k) The pressure at any point in a free-standing liquid is DIRECTLY PROPORTIONAL to its depth below the surface. (22) A is three times as far below the surface as B.

∴ The pressure at point A is three times as great as the pressure at point B. The pressure at point B is NOT three times as great as the pressure at point A.

EXERCISE A *Contextual reference*

1. In sentence 2, *It* refers to:
   (a) The container
   (b) The bottom of the container
   (c) A liquid
2. In sentence 3, *this* refers to:
   (a) The carton of milk
   (b) The fact that the sides of the carton curve outwards
3. In sentence 4, *they* refers to:
   (a) Wooden barrels
   (b) Wooden barrels and water tanks
   (c) Metal bands
4. In sentence 6, *these objects* refers to:
   (a) A rubber ball and a plastic boat
   (b) Containers
   (c) A rubber ball, a plastic boat and a container

5. In sentence 12, *the object* refers to:
   (a) The table mentioned in sentence 10
   (b) The block of metal mentioned in sentence 10
   (c) The object mentioned in sentence 11
6. In sentence 14, *it* refers to:
   (a) The surface
   (b) The area of the surface
   (c) The force
7. In sentence 17, *this* refers to:
   (a) The other surface of the object
   (b) The object
8. In sentence 22, *its* refers to:
   (a) The pressure
   (b) The point
   (c) The free-standing liquid

EXERCISE B *Rephrasing*

Rewrite the following sentences replacing the words printed in italics with expressions from the text which have the same meaning.
1. Water *presses* on the sides and bottom of the container in which it rests.
2. Wooden barrels are usually *reinforced* with metal bands.
3. A liquid exerts *a force upwards* as well as *a force downwards*.
4. *We measure a force* in newtons.
5. The pressure *which an object exerts* does not depend only on its weight.
6. *Pressure is measured* by the force divided by *the area of the surface on which it acts*.
7. An object *which weighs* 5 N exerts a force of 5 N.

EXERCISE C *Relationships between statements*

Place the following expressions in the sentences indicated. Replace and re-order the words in the sentence where necessary.

(a) that is to say (2)	(g) but (9)	(m) then (17)
(b) because of (3)	(h) however (12)	(n) although (18)
(c) for example (3)	(i) because (12+13)	(o) then (20)
(d) in order to (4)	(j) then (14)	(p) however (21)
(e) for example (6)	(k) for example (15)	(q) therefore (23)
(f) then (7)	(l) then (16)	(r) consequently (23)

EXERCISE D *Classifications and generalizations*

1. Draw the following diagram and complete it by filling in the spaces.

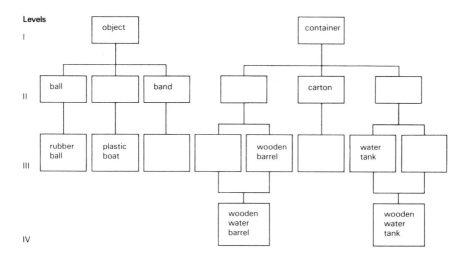

2. The different levels in the diagram are *levels of generalization*. Items at the higher level are more general than items at the lower level. The diagrams are *classifications*. Items at a lower level are kinds or *classes* of items at a higher level. Thus:

A ball is a kind of object.

Balls, boats and bands are kinds of object.

A barrel is a kind of container.

Barrels, cartons and tanks are kinds of container.

Classify the following items in the form of diagrams.

EXAMPLE

Metal container, jar, tin can, test-tube, glass container, container

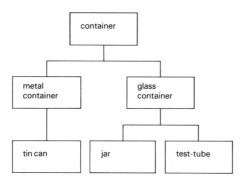

(a) substance, gas, liquid, solid, wood, ice, oxygen
(b) metric unit, non-metric unit, weight unit, ton, kilogram, pound, gram, stone
(c) barometer, thermometer, ammeter, measuring instrument, cutting instrument, instrument

(d) nitrogen, visible gas, chlorine, hydrogen, invisible gas, gas
(e) ferrous metal, zinc, iron, lead, metal, non-ferrous metal, steel
(f) acid, base, sodium chloride, copper sulphate, compound, salt, sodium hydroxide, nitric acid
(g) sulphuric acid, substance, acid, carbonic acid, inorganic acid, acetic acid, organic acid, citric acid
(h) solid, cube, cylinder, regular solid, irregular solid, pyramid

3. Use the diagrams you have drawn to write out classifications and examples of the following form:

EXAMPLE

Substances can/may be classified as gases, liquids and solids.
or Substances can/may be divided into three classes: gases, liquids and solids. Wood and ice are examples of solids and steam is an example of a gas. *or* Wood and ice, for example, are solids and steam is a gas.

4. Statements which use higher level items are more general than statements which use lower level items. The following statements, for example, get less and less general:

(i) Metals expand when heated.
(ii) Ferrous metals expand when heated.
(iii) Steel expands when heated.
(iv) Pieces of steel expand when heated.
(v) Railway lines expand in hot weather.
If (i) is true, then (ii), (iii), (iv) and (v) are all true.
Change the following statements into higher level generalizations, *where possible.*

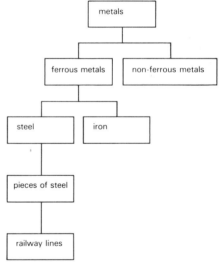

(a) Water exerts a force on the bottom of the container in which it rests.
(b) Copper expands when heated.
(c) Dibasic acids contain two atoms of hydrogen replaceable by a metal.
(d) Nitric acid consists of hydrogen and an acid radical.
(e) The volume of a pyramid can be calculated by a mathematical formula.
(f) Citric acid is found in lemons and oranges.
(g) The pressure exerted by a block of metal depends on the area of contact.
(h) A barometer measures atmospheric pressure.
(i) Air occupies space and has weight.
(j) Ice may be changed into water and water into steam.

5. Use the statements given in 4 and the generalizations you have derived from them to make sets of statements of the following form:

EXAMPLE
A liquid exerts a force on the bottom of the container in which it rests. Water is a liquid.
Therefore (∴) water exerts a force on the bottom of the container in which it rests.

II PROBLEMS
INFORMATION TRANSFER

A. (1) DIRECTIONS
Take a tall container of some kind.
Make several holes at different heights along the side of the container.
Place the container on the bench next to a sink so that the holes face towards the sink.
Fill the container with water.

(2) STATEMENT OF RESULT
A curved stream of water comes from each hole, but the streams from the lower holes extend straighter and further than the streams from the upper holes.

(3) CONCLUSION
This shows that . . .

Draw the diagram below and complete it so as to illustrate the result of this experiment.

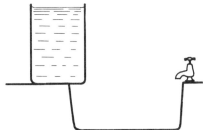

Write out a *description* of this experiment. Refer to Problem C, Unit 3.

B. Use the information in the following diagrams to make statements about the pressure exerted by solid objects. Begin with a *generalization*, and then show how each of the diagrams illustrates it.

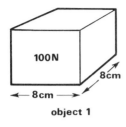

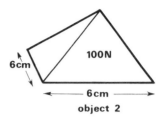

object 1   object 2

C. Use the information in the following diagram to make statements about liquid pressure. Begin with a *generalization* and then give the pressure at each of the points marked in order to illustrate the generalization.

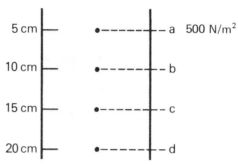

III GRAMMAR
EXERCISE A *Short-form relative clauses*

(a) We have seen (Unit 3) that if two sentences each contain a noun phrase, and the noun phrases refer to the same thing, then the sentences can be joined together by a relative pronoun like *which*.

EXAMPLE
  (a) 40 per cent of the houses had inadequate earths.
  (b) The houses were surveyed by the Electricity Board.
  = 40 per cent of the houses *which were surveyed by the Electricity Board* had inadequate earths.

(b) If the relative clause contains a passive verb, the clause can be shortened by omitting *which*+verb 'to be'.

EXAMPLE
    40 per cent of the houses *which were surveyed by the Electricity Board* had inadequate earths.
  = 40 per cent of the houses *surveyed by the Electricity Board* had inadequate earths.

(c) Combine each of the following pairs of sentences into a single sentence. Make the second sentence into a *short-form relative clause* and insert it into the first sentence at the place marked by the dots. Note in each case whether the relative clause is defining or non-defining.

EXAMPLE

The heat . . . is produced by an electric arc.

The heat is required for welding.

The heat *required for welding* is produced by an electric arc (defining).

1. The solution . . . is said to be neutral, since it does not turn blue litmus red or turn red litmus blue. The solution is formed as a result of the above process.

2. The method is similar to that . . . , as the following experiment will indicate. That was described on p. 246.

3. One variety of iron ore, . . . , consists mainly of iron (III) oxide, Fe_2O_3. This variety is known as haematite.

4. The white solid . . . is the salt ammonium chloride which is formed by direct combination of the two gases. The white solid is formed in this action. (There are two relative clauses in this sentence. Underline them both in your notebook. Which clause is defining and which non-defining?)

5. Many substances . . . are not bleached by exposure to ordinary oxygen. These substances are bleached by moist chlorine.

6. At this point we must turn our attention to the carbon . . . . Carbon is found in green plants.

7. Galvanized iron, . . . , consists of iron sheets which have been given a thin coating of zinc. Galvanized iron is often used in the form of corrugated sheets for roofing. (There are two relative clauses in this sentence. Underline them both in your notebook. Which clause is defining and which non-defining?)

8. The carbon monoxide . . . makes the gas very poisonous. The carbon monoxide is introduced during the process.

9. The ordinary sugar . . . is called cane sugar, as most of it used to be manufactured from sugar-cane. Ordinary sugar is used at table.*

10. Solutions of zinc chloride, $ZnCl_2$, . . . , are used by tinsmiths for cleaning the surfaces of metals before soldering. Solutions of zinc chloride are made by dissolving scrap zinc in hydrochloric acid.

11. Chemists can build up from simple substances many of the complex substances . . . , but they have not succeeded in building up living bodies from non-living matter. The complex substances are found in plant and animal bodies.

12. We can show the pressure . . . by means of the following experiment. The pressure is exerted by the atmosphere.

* Note *used* to be manufactured, pronounced ju:st
  used at table, pronounced ju:zd

EXERCISE B *Noun compounds*

If we want to describe an object in greater detail or at a lower level of generalization (see Section I, Exercise D), we may use an adjective:

water – *hot* water
a fire – an *electric* fire
a liquid – a *cloudy* liquid

We can also put a noun in front of a noun:

a cylinder – a *steel* cylinder
a pump – a *bicycle* pump
a filter – an *air* filter

Many grammatical relationships are possible in Noun+Noun constructions, or *noun compounds*. They can be shown by *paraphrases*.

EXAMPLES

Noun Compounds	Paraphrases
steam engine	= engine which works by steam
cardboard carton	= carton (which is) made of cardboard
milk carton	= carton which contains milk
pocket torch	= torch which can go in a pocket
(etc.)	

Write down *paraphrases* which will show the 'grammatical meaning' of the following noun compounds:

copper electrode	suction pump
friction brake	iron filings
boiling point	horseshoe magnet
cooling tower	test tube
spring balance	plant parasite
iodine solution	density bottle
glass jar	filter paper
gas jar	nickel alloy
bell jar	extraction pump
mercury column	chalk soil
mercury poisoning	combustion chamber
condensation losses	gas oven
electron theory	Wheatstone bridge

IV   PARAGRAPH WRITING
STAGE 1 *Sentence building*

Join each of the twelve groups of words below into one sentence using the additional material at the beginning of each group. Omit words in italics. Number your sentences and begin each one with a capital letter.

1 BY/BORING/AND/FILLING
   this can be done *in the following way*
   we bore holes at different levels through the side of a tin can
   we fill the can with water

2 ,/,
   water *is* like all liquids
   water exerts a downwards force

3 WHEN/CONTAINING/,/THAN/WHEN/, AND/AS
   a bucket *contains* water
   the bucket is lifted up
   it is heavier to hold
   it is empty
   its weight increases
   more water is poured in*to the bucket*

4 ONE/IS/THE/OF
   this is an example
   we supply water for ordinary domestic *purposes*
   people use *this water**

5 THE/IN ANY HOUSE/BETWEEN THE HOUSE AND THE SUPPLY
   water pressure depends on the difference in level

6 ,/WHICH/TO
   the source of our water supply is rain
   rain accumulates in reservoirs
   the reservoirs are specially built
   the reservoirs hold a large quantity of water

7 , AND/,/WHICH/PREVENTING IT/FROM FALLING
   the total weight is acting vertically downwards
   the weight of the water is acting on the bottom of the bucket
   the bottom of the bucket is *stopping the water*
   the water does not fall any further

8 THAT/CONTAINING
   we can show *this* quite easily
   liquids exert a pressure on the sides of a vessel
   the vessel contains a liquid

9 AND/, THOUGH/IN ANY PART OF THE HOUSE/TO
   the pressure is lowest on the top floor
   the pressure is highest in the basement
   usually the pressure is sufficient
   the pressure will ensure a satisfactory supply

  * Note: *use* (verb) pronounced ju:z
       use (noun) pronounced ju:s

10   THERE ARE/WHEN/THE/THAT
     many instances *occur* in everyday life
     use is made of *this* fact
     liquids exert a pressure

11   FOR PURIFICATION,/AND/,/WHICH
     from the reservoir the water goes to filter beds
     the water is purified
     then *the water goes* to the main water pipe
     the pipe carries water to the houses

12   , AND/IT/THAN/THOSE/,/SHOWING THAT/AS
     the water spurts out horizontally from the holes
     the water will spurt out much further from *some* holes
     these holes are near the bottom of the can
     the water will not spurt very far from *the other holes*
     these holes are near the top *of the can*
     the pressure increases
     the depth increases

STAGE 2 *Paragraph building*

Rewrite the twelve sentences in a logical order to make a paragraph. Before
you write the paragraph, add the following material:
     write 'thus' at the beginning of sentence 2
     write 'also' after 'can' in sentence 8.
When you have written your paragraph, re-read it and make sure that the
sentences are presented in a logical order. Give the paragraph a suitable
title. Compare your paragraph with the relevant paragraph in the Free Reading passage. Make any changes that you think are necessary, but remember
that sentences can often be arranged in more than one way.

STAGE 3 *Paragraph reconstruction*

Read through the paragraph again. Make sure you know all the words, using
a dictionary if necessary. Without referring to your previous work rewrite
the paragraph. Here are some notes to help you.
     bucket containing water – heavier than when empty – weight increases–
          more water
     total weight – acting downwards – weight of water – acting on bottom of
          bucket – preventing it from falling
     water – exerts downward force
     show easily – liquids exert pressure – sides of vessel
     bore holes – different levels – fill can
     water spurts – further from holes near bottom – pressure increases – depth
          increases
     everyday life – use made of fact – liquids exert pressure

supply of water – domestic use
source = rain – accumulates in reservoirs – large quantity of water
to filter beds – to main water pipe – to houses
water pressure – difference in level – house and supply
lowest on top floor – highest in basement – usually sufficient – satisfactory
   supply

V   FREE READING

Read the following passage in your own time. Try to find additional examples of the points you have studied in this and other Units.

When a bucket containing water is lifted up, it is heavier to hold than when it is empty, and its weight increases as more water is poured in. The total weight is acting vertically downwards, and the weight of the water is acting on the bottom of the bucket, which is preventing it from falling any further. Thus water, like all liquids, exerts a downward force. We can also show quite easily that liquids exert a pressure on the sides of a containing vessel. This can be done by boring holes at different levels through the sides of a tin can and filling the can with water. The water spurts out horizontally from the holes, and it will spurt out much further from holes near the bottom of the can than from those near the top, showing that the pressure increases as the depth increases. There are many instances in everyday life where use is made of the fact that liquids exert a pressure. One example is the supply of water for ordinary domestic use. The source of our water supply is rain, which accumulates in reservoirs specially built to hold a large quantity of water. From the reservoir the water goes to filter beds for purification, and then to the main water pipe, which carries water to the houses. The water pressure in any house depends on the difference in level between the house and the supply. The pressure is lowest on the top floor and highest in the basement, though usually the pressure in any part of a house is sufficient to ensure a satisfactory supply.

   If a liquid is poured into a set of communicating vessels it rises to the same height in each, even though the vessels have very different sizes and shapes. The principle that balanced columns of the same liquid always rise to the same height is utilized in the construction of a town water supply. Ideally the reservoir should be located on high ground with the result that the water flows through the pipes to any point which is not higher than the water level in the reservoir. Under certain circumstances water may be made to rise considerably above ground level from artesian wells (the name derives from Artois, a province in France, where this method of obtaining a water supply was first practised). The operation of an artesian well is illustrated in Diagram 1:

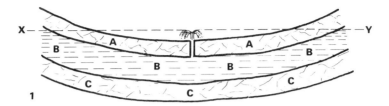

1

A and C are saucer-shaped layers of rock which will not allow water to soak through them. These two impermeable layers are separated by a layer of porous rock B which becomes filled with water to the level XY. If a boring is made through A as shown, the water will gush up through the hole and will rise in pipes until it reaches the level of the main body of water, XY.

Diagram 2 illustrates the principle of the hydraulic press, which is used in working lifts, forging steel, and in processes for making highly compressed bales of wool, paper or straw:

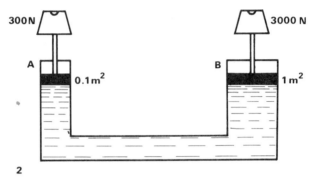

2

A hydraulic press is a device for securing mechanical advantage from the pressures of liquid columns. In its simplest form it consists of a wide cylinder and a narrow cylinder connected by a tube. Both cylinders are filled with water and fitted with a piston. Since the pressures at points at the same level in a liquid are equal, if the piston at A exerts a pressure of 300 N/m^2 on the water, the water will exert an equal pressure on the piston at B, and therefore exert a force of 3,000 N on the 1 m² area of B. In other words, a mass of 30 kg placed on A will support a load of 300 kg on B. The mechanical advantage is calculated by dividing the area of the large piston by the area of the small piston. The mechanical advantage of the hydraulic press in Diagram 2 ,therefore, is $\dfrac{10}{1} = 10$.

5 Magnets

[1]A magnet is a substance which attracts certain other substances. [2]A substance which is attracted by a magnet can itself be made into a magnet.

[3]Generally speaking, there are three substances which are attracted by a magnet: iron, cobalt and nickel. [4]Substances which are attracted by a magnet are known as magnetic substances, and those which are not are referred to as non-magnetic substances. [5]Iron, cobalt and nickel are magnetic substances. [6]They are attracted by magnets and they can themselves be magnetized.

[7]Mixtures of metals, or alloys, which contain a magnetic substance generally also have magnetic properties. [8]Some alloys containing none of the above metals, however, are also magnetic. [9]Certain alloys containing manganese, aluminium and copper belong to this class. [10]They are magnetic, even though they contain no metal which is itself magnetic.

(a) A magnet attracts other substances.
(b) Iron, cobalt and nickel are the three substances which are attracted by a magnet.
(c) Cobalt can be made into a magnet.
(d) Alloys which contain a magnetic substance are always magnetic.
(e) Manganese is a non-magnetic substance.
(f) Alloys containing aluminium are magnetic.

[11]A magnet will attract a magnetic substance like iron. [12]Not all parts of a magnet, however, have equal attractive force. [13]If a bar magnet is placed in iron filings, most of the filings will stick to the ends of the magnet, and very few will adhere to the central part. [14]The force of attraction, or magnetic force, is concentrated near the ends of the magnet. [15]These areas are known as the poles.

[16]A magnet sets in a definite direction when freely suspended. [17]If a bar magnet is suspended by a thread and allowed to move freely, it will come to rest with one pole pointing towards the south. [18]The pole pointing towards

the north is called the north-seeking, or north, pole; and that which points towards the south the south-seeking, or south, pole.

(g)   The central part of a bar magnet has no magnetic force.

(h)   Most of the magnetic force in a magnet is near the poles.

[19]If the north poles of two freely suspended magnets are brought into proximity, so that they are close together, the ends of the two magnets will swing away from each other. [20]If on the other hand the north pole of one magnet is brought close to the south pole of the other, the two ends will attract each other. [21]A north pole will attract a south pole and repel another north pole, and be attracted by a south pole and repelled by another north pole. [22]Like poles repel one another and unlike poles attract one another.

(i)   A south pole will attract a north pole.

(j)   A north pole and a south pole are like poles.

(k)   Two magnets freely suspended will swing away from each other when they are brought close together.

Solutions

(a)   A magnet attracts other substances.

=   A magnet attracts ALL other substances.

but   A magnet is a substance which attracts CERTAIN (i.e. some but not all) other substances. (1)

∴   It is NOT TRUE that a magnet attracts (all) other substances.

(b)   Iron, cobalt and nickel are THE three substances which are attracted by a magnet.

=   Iron, cobalt and nickel are the ONLY three substances which are attracted by a magnet.

but   GENERALLY SPEAKING, there are three substances which are attracted by a magnet. (3)

i.e.   There may be other substances which are attracted by a magnet.

e.g.   Some alloys containing none of the above metals are magnetic. (8)
        An alloy is a substance.

∴   It is NOT TRUE that iron, cobalt and nickel are the (only) three substances which are attracted by a magnet.

(c)   Iron, cobalt and nickel are magnetic substances. (5)
        Magnetic substances are substances which are attracted by a magnet. (4)

∴   Cobalt is attracted by a magnet.
        A substance which is attracted by a magnet can itself be made into a magnet. (2)

∴   *Cobalt can be made into a magnet.*

(d) Alloys which contain a magnetic substance GENERALLY (i.e. not always) have magnetic properties. (7)
have magnetic properties = are magnetic
∴ It is NOT TRUE that alloys which contain a magnetic substance are always magnetic.

(e) Some alloys containing none of the metals iron, cobalt or nickel are magnetic. (3, 8)
Iron, cobalt and nickel are magnetic substances. (3, 4)
Certain alloys containing manganese, aluminium and copper are magnetic even though they contain no metal which is itself magnetic. (9, 10)
i.e. Alloys containing manganese, aluminium and copper contain substances which are not magnetic (i.e. non-magnetic substances).
∴ *Manganese is a non-magnetic substance.*

(f) Alloys containing aluminium are magnetic.
= ALL alloys which contain aluminium are magnetic.
CERTAIN (i.e. not all) alloys which contain aluminium are magnetic. (8, 9)
∴ It is NOT TRUE that (all) alloys containing aluminium are magnetic.

(g) If a bar magnet is placed in iron filings, VERY FEW (of the filings) will adhere to the central part. (13)
i.e. SOME filings will adhere to the central part.
∴ The central part of the magnet has SOME magnetic force.
∴ It is NOT TRUE that the central part of a bar magnet has no magnetic force.

(h) The magnetic force is concentrated near the ends of the magnet. (14)
i.e. Most of the magnetic force is near the ends of the magnet.
The ends of the magnet are known as the poles. (15)
∴ Most of the magnetic force is near the poles of the magnet.
= *Most of the magnetic force in a magnet is near the poles.*

(i) A north pole will be attracted by a south pole. (21)
= *A south pole will attract a north pole.*

(j) A north pole will attract a south pole . . . and be attracted by a south pole. (21)
Unlike poles attract one another. (22)
∴ A north pole and a south pole are UNLIKE poles.

(k) Two magnets . . . will swing away from each other
= Two magnets . . . will ALWAYS swing away from each other.
Like poles repel one another and unlike poles attract one another. (22)

∴   Two magnets will swing away from each other ONLY IF the two like poles are brought close together.

∴   It is NOT TRUE that two magnets freely suspended will (always) swing away from each other when they are brought close together.

EXERCISE A *Contextual reference*

1. In sentence 8, *the above metals* refers to:
   (a) Iron, cobalt and nickel
   (b) Alloys
2. In sentence 9, *this class* refers to:
   (a) The class of alloys which contain a magnetic substance.
   (b) The class of alloys which contain no iron, cobalt or nickel but are magnetic.
   (c) The class of alloys which contain manganese, aluminium and copper.
3. In sentence 10, *they* refers to:
   (a) Manganese, aluminium and copper
   (b) Certain alloys containing manganese, aluminium and copper.
4. In sentence 15, *these areas* refers to:
   (a) The force of attraction, or magnetic force
   (b) The ends of the magnet
5. In sentence 19, *they* refers to:
   (a) The north poles
   (b) The two magnets

EXERCISE B *Rephrasing*

Rewrite the following sentences replacing the words printed in italics with expressions from the text which have the same meaning.

1. A substance which is attracted by a magnet can itself be *made into a magnet*.
2. Substances which are not attracted by a magnet *are referred to as* non-magnetic substances.
3. Generally speaking, *mixtures of metals* which contain a magnetic substance *have magnetic properties*.
4. Alloys *which contain* iron, cobalt or nickel are generally magnetic.
5. If a bar magnet is placed in iron filings, most of the filings will *stick* to the ends of the magnet.
6. The *force of attraction* of a magnet is concentrated near the *ends of the magnet*.
7. *A magnet which is freely suspended* sets in a definite direction.
8. If the *north poles* of two magnets are *brought into proximity with* each other, they will repel each other.
9. The pole *pointing* towards the north *is called* the *north-seeking* pole.
10. *A north pole will be attracted by a south pole.*

EXERCISE C *Relationships between statements*

Place the following expressions in the sentences indicated. Replace and re-order the words in the sentences where necessary.

(a) may be defined as (1)
(b) furthermore (2)
(c) therefore (5)
(d) that is to say (6)
(e) but (7+8)

(f) although (7+8)
(g) for example (9)
(h) that is to say (10)
(i) then (11)
(j) although (11+12)
(p) thus (22)

(k) for example (13)
(l) thus (14)
(m) for example (17)
(n) however (20)
(o) then (21)

EXERCISE D *Inductive statements*

Refer to the Problems Sections in Units 1, 3 and 4 and study the following diagram:

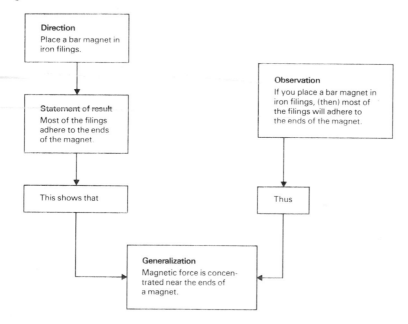

Making a *generalization* on the basis of an *observation* is known as an *induction*.

1. Using the above diagram as a guide, make inductions from the following experiments. Note that in some cases the generalization follows more than one observation.

(a) Suspend a bar magnet by a thread and allow it to move freely. It comes to rest with one pole pointing towards the north and the other pointing towards the south.
A magnet sets in a definite direction when freely suspended.

58   *English in Physical Science*

(b) Suspend two bar magnets by separate threads.
Bring the north poles of the two magnets close together.
The ends of the two magnets swing away from each other.
Like poles repel each other.

(c) Suspend two bar magnets by separate threads.
Bring the north poles of the two magnets close together.
The ends of the two magnets swing away from each other.
Bring the north pole of one magnet close to the south pole of the other magnet.
The two ends attract each other.
Like poles repel each other and unlike poles attract each other.

(d) Take an oblong object weighing 200 N with one surface area of 200 cm^2 and another of 100 cm^2 and place it on a table so that the area of contact is 200 cm^2.
The pressure exerted by the object is 200 N/200 cm^2 = 10,000 N/m^2.
Place the object on the table so that the area of contact is 100 cm^2.
The pressure exerted by the object is 200 N/100 cm^2 = 20,000 N/m^2.
Pressure is measured by the force divided by the area of the surface on which it acts (see Unit 4).

(e) Make several holes at different heights along the side of a tall container.
Fill the container with water.
A curved stream of water comes from each hole, but the streams from the lower holes extend straighter and further than the streams from the upper holes.
Water pressure increases with depth (see Problem A, Unit 4).

(f) Push a rubber ball under the surface of the water in a container.
You feel an upward force against the bottom of the ball.
Water exerts a pressure upwards (see Unit 4).

2. There is more than one way of expressing an observation.

EXAMPLE
    (a) If *you place a bar magnet* in iron filings, then most of the filings will adhere to the ends of the magnet.
= (b) If *a bar magnet is placed* in iron filings, then most of the filings will adhere to the ends of the magnet.
= (c) If a bar magnet is placed in iron filings, most of the filings adhere to the ends of the magnet.

Express the observations in the inductions you have made in 1 above in different ways.

3. There is more than one way of expressing the fact that a given generalization follows from a given observation.

EXAMPLE

   (a) If you place a bar magnet in iron filings, most of the filings will adhere to the ends of the magnet. *Thus* magnetic force is concentrated near the ends of a magnet.

= (b) If you place a bar magnet in iron filings, most of the filings will adhere to the ends of the magnet. Magnetic force, *then*, is concentrated near the ends of a magnet.

= (c) If you place a bar magnet in iron filings, most of the filings will adhere to the ends of the magnet. *It follows that* magnetic force is concentrated near the ends of a magnet.

= (d) If you place a bar magnet in iron filings, most of the filings will adhere to the ends of the magnet. Magnetic force, *therefore*, is concentrated near the ends of a magnet.

= (e) If you place a bar magnet in iron filings, most of the filings will adhere to the ends of the magnet. *Hence* magnetic force is concentrated near the ends of a magnet.

Express the inductions you have made in 1 above in different ways by replacing *thus* with *then, it follows that, therefore, hence.*

EXERCISE E *Deductive statements and illustrations*

1. Making a generalization first and relating it to an observation is known as *deduction.*

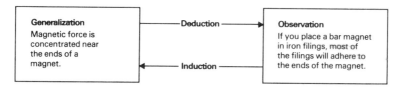

Change the inductions you have made in 1, 2 and 3 above into deductions.

EXAMPLE

Induction

If you place a bar magnet in iron filings, most of the filings adhere to the ends of the magnet. *Thus (Hence, It follows that* etc.) magnetic force is concentrated near the ends of a magnet.

Deduction

Magnetic force is concentrated near the ends of a magnet. *Thus (Hence, It follows that* etc.) if you place a bar magnet in iron filings, most of the filings cling to the ends of the magnet.

2. Observations which follow generalizations are often used as *illustrations.*

EXAMPLE

Magnetic force is concentrated near the ends of a magnet. If, *for example,* you place a bar magnet in iron filings, most of the filings adhere to the ends of the magnet.

Change the deductions you have made in Exercise E, 1 above into generalizations+illustrations. Note that the passive can also be used.

II PROBLEMS
INFORMATION TRANSFER

DIAGRAMS BASED ON STATEMENTS

A. Draw diagrams to illustrate the following statements:

(i) A freely suspended bar magnet will come to rest with one pole pointing towards the north and the other pointing towards the south.

(ii) If a bar magnet is placed in iron filings, most of the filings will cling to the ends of the magnet, and very few to the central part.

(iii) A north pole will attract a south pole and repel another north pole, and be attracted by a south pole and repelled by another north pole.

B. Complete the following:

(1) DIRECTIONS

Take two cylindrical bar magnets of equal length.

Place them close to each other on a flat surface so that the north poles and the south poles are at the same ends.

(2) STATEMENT OF RESULT

The two magnets roll . . .

(3) CONCLUSION

This shows that . . . (+generalization)

(1) DIRECTIONS

Turn one of the magnets round so that the north pole of one is at the same end as the south pole of the other.

(2) STATEMENT OF RESULT

. . . .

(3) CONCLUSION

This shows that . . . (+generalization)

Use the above information to make

(a) an induction,

(b) a deduction

(c) a generalization+illustration

Draw diagrams to illustrate this experiment.

III GRAMMAR

EXERCISE A *Relative clauses with prepositions*

(a) In scientific writing we find many relative clauses with a preposition before *which*. Such clauses are formed in the following way:

The production of a gas—substances would burn more fiercely *in this gas* than in air—was discovered by Joseph Priestley in 1774.

= The production of a gas *in which* substances would burn more fiercely than in air was discovered by Joseph Priestley in 1774.

(b) Rewrite the following sentences so that they contain relative clauses beginning with a preposition+which:

1. A substance which alters the rate—an action takes place at this rate—without itself being used up in the action is said to act as a catalyst or to bring about catalysis.
2. A bee-hive shelf has a hole in its side—the tube passes through this hole—and one in the top—the gas passes into the jar through this hole.
3. Mention has already been made of the importance of air in connection with the processes—life depends on these processes.
4. It is obvious that when water is boiled the steam formed occupies a much greater volume than the water—it was formed from this water.
5. If the temperature falls to a point lower than the one—the vapour present would cause saturation at this temperature—some of the vapour will condense.
6. Other crystals—water of crystallization can be driven from these crystals—are those of washing soda and Epsom salts, but it must not be assumed that all crystals contain water.
7. The results of this experiment suggest that when an electric current passes through the coils the pieces of iron—they are wrapped round these pieces of iron—act as magnets.
8. The ancients realized that the fixed stars formed readily recognizable groups, known as constellations—they gave names often based on fancied resemblances to animals or objects to these groups.
9. When the flow of water ceases the vessel will be filled just to the top of the pipe—a measuring jar is then placed below this pipe.
10. Just inside the wall of a plant cell there is a layer of material known as protoplasm—there is a denser object called the nucleus of the cell inside this layer of material.
11. The connecting pipes and the hot-water tank—heat should not escape from the pipes and the tank—are wrapped in felt to prevent conduction from them.
12. Since the temperature of an object is a measure of the average kinetic energy of the molecules of the object, the absolute zero represents the tem-

perature—the kinetic energy is zero at this temperature—, that is, the temperature—the molecules are completely at rest at this temperature.

EXERCISE B *The present participle and past participle as modifiers*

(a) Apart from the simple adjectives in everyday use (*cold* water, *blue* litmus, a *new* substance) scientists use a large number of *modifiers* made up of a verb root+suffix. Two important classes of modifiers are as follows:

(i) *Present participle modifiers*
   Modifiers formed from verbs by adding -*ing* (present participles).

EXAMPLE
   lubricate+*ing* → *lubricating*
   lubricating oil = oil which *lubricates* something

(ii) *Past participle modifiers*
   Modifiers formed from verbs by using the appropriate past participle form (*saturated, purified, given, made*, etc.)

EXAMPLE
   lubricate+*ed* → *lubricated*
   a *lubricated* bearing = a bearing which *has been lubricated.*

(b) Complete the following sentences, filling in the gaps with a *present participle modifier* or a *past participle modifier*. Form each modifier from one of the verbs in the list:

saturate	predetermine
result	polish
rotate	oxidize
condense	live
compress	invert
purify	burn
blacken	

1. The . . . air forces its way between the rubber and the metal tube through the hole, and so into the tyre.
2. Protoplasm is the . . . matter of a cell.
3. In hot climates the surface layers of rocks are rapidly heated by the sunshine in the day-time and the . . . expansion helps to break up the rocks.
4. An . . . siphon is used to form a seal for preventing the flow of sewer gas back into the house.
5. A . . . solution of a common salt boils at 109°C.
6. The . . . blades whirl the water towards the outside of the blades whence it leaves through the discharge pipe.
7. . . . milk is prepared by abstracting some of the water from liquid milk by boiling it in a partial vacuum.
8. A . . . surface is a poor reflector of heat, but a brightly . . . surface is a good reflector.

9. Coal is heated in large iron retorts and the gas which issues from it is subjected to a number of . . . processes to remove the ammonia it contains.
10. It appears that air contains at least two different kinds of gas, one of which combines with . . . magnesium while the other extinguishes . . . substances.
11. Petrol from the fuel tank enters the float chamber of the carburettor and fills it up to a . . . level, generally slightly below the level of the jet.
12. The . . . test shows that hydrogen escapes upwards more easily than downwards, and so it must be less dense than air.

IV PARAGRAPH WRITING

STAGE 1 *Sentence building*

Join each of the ten groups of words below into one sentence, using the additional material at the beginning of each group. Omit words in italics. Number your sentences and begin each one with a capital letter.

1 MAGNETIZED/SO THAT/UPRIGHT/WITH/PROTRUDING/, AND/
   HORIZONTALLY
   Place a knitting needle in a cork
   it will float in a trough of water
   its north pole *will* just *protrude* out of the cork
   support a bar magnet above the water

2 THAT/;/(1791–1867)/TO/OF/WHAT/SURROUNDING
   it is important to realize *this*
   lines of force have no objective existence
   they were suggested by Michael Faraday
   they give a mental picture
   something is happening in the space
   the space surrounds a magnet

3 FLOATING/WITH ITS/AND/IT
   put the needle *near the magnet*
   the north pole *of the needle will be* near the north pole of the magnet
   release *the needle*

4 THE EXISTENCE OF/BY A SIMPLE EXPERIMENT
   lines of force *exist*
   this may be demonstrated

5 TO THE SOUTH POLE OF THE MAGNET
   the needle will travel along a curved path

6 TO/DIFFERENT/, AND/SO
   a diagram can be drawn
   the diagram will represent the paths
   the paths are traced out by the needle
   the lines *are* drawn
   the lines indicate lines of magnetic force

7 ; THAT IS,/TEND TO/WHICH
   the forces act along definite lines
   magnetic poles will be driven along certain lines
   these lines are called lines of force

8 AS/AN INDEPENDENT/WHEN/IT/FREE TO MOVE
   we can define a line of magnetic force
   a line of magnetic force is the path *of a needle*
   the path is traced out by *a* north pole
   the north pole is under the influence of a magnet

9 THE/ROUND A MAGNET/CALLED
   this area is a magnetic field

10 IF/WITH/,/ALWAYS/, BUT
   the experiment is repeated
   the needle *will be* in different starting positions
   the starting positions will be near the north pole of the magnet
   the needle will travel to the south pole
   the needle will travel along different paths

STAGE 2 *Paragraph building*

Rewrite the ten sentences in a logical order to make a paragraph. Before you
write the paragraph, add the following material:
   write 'within this field' at the beginning of sentence 7.
   When you have written your paragraph, re-read it and make sure that the
sentences are presented in a logical order. Give the paragraph a suitable title.
Compare your paragraph with the relevant paragraph in the Free Reading
passage. Make any changes that you think are necessary, but remember that
sentences can often be arranged in more than one way.

STAGE 3 *Paragraph reconstruction*

Read through the paragraph again. Make sure you know all the words,
using a dictionary if necessary. Without referring to your previous work rewrite the paragraph. Here are some notes to help you.
   area round a magnet – magnetic field
   forces act along definite lines – magnetic poles – driven along lines – lines
      of force
   existence – demonstrated – simple experiment

knitting needle – cork – float upright – north pole protruding – bar magnet
– above water

needle – north pole of magnet – release it

needle – travel – south pole of magnet – curved path

repeated – different starting positions – north pole of magnet – to south
pole – different paths

diagram – represent different paths – moving needle – lines of magnetic
force

define a line of magnetic force as . . .

important – no objective existence – Faraday – mental picture – space
surrounding a magnet

V FREE READING

Read the following passage in your own time. Try to find additional examples
of the points you have studied in this and other Units.

Some of the properties of magnets were known from very early times.
For example, it was known over 2,000 years ago that the mineral magnetite,
an oxide of iron, possesses the property of attracting iron. The Chinese,
earlier than 2,500 B.C., knew that if a piece of magnetite is suspended so
that it can turn freely in a horizontal plane it will set in a definite direction
and can therefore be used as a primitive compass. Later it was found that
if a bar of iron is rubbed with a piece of magnetite, or lodestone, the
magnetic properties of the lodestone are transferred to the iron. The
lodestone is called a natural magnet as distinct from other types of magnet
which are made by various artificial processes.

Magnets today are usually made of special alloys of steel. A steel magnet
differs from ordinary steel and from all other substances in three important
respects: it attracts iron filings, it sets in a definite direction when freely
suspended, and it converts iron and steel bars in its neighbourhood into
magnets. If we place a bar-magnet in iron filings it will emerge with a
cluster of filings attached to each end, showing that there is a centre of
magnetic force at each end of the bar. These centres are called the poles
of the magnet. A bar-magnet suspended horizontally in a paper stirrup
will always set with the line joining its poles along a north and south line;
in other words, the magnet has a north-seeking pole and a south-seeking
pole. A bar-magnet floating on a cork will set roughly north and south
but it will not move either to the north or to the south, showing that the
two poles are equal in strength. If we bring the north pole of one magnet
close to the south pole of another magnet, the unlike poles attract one
another, but if we bring two north poles or two south poles into proximity
we find that like poles repel one another.

The area round a magnet is called a magnetic field. Within this field the forces act along definite lines; that is, magnetic poles will tend to be driven along certain lines which are called lines of force. The existence of lines of force may be demonstrated by a simple experiment. Place a magnetized knitting needle in a cork so that it will float upright in a trough of water, with its north pole just protruding out of the cork, and support a bar magnet horizontally above the water. Put the floating needle with its north pole near the north pole of the magnet and release it. The needle will travel to the south pole of the magnet along a curved path. If the experiment is repeated with the needle in different starting positions near the north pole of the magnet, the needle will always travel to the south pole, but along different paths. A diagram can be drawn to represent the different paths traced out by the needle, and the lines so drawn indicate lines of magnetic force. We can define a line of magnetic force as the path traced out by an independent north pole when it is free to move under the influence of a magnet. It is important to realize that lines of force have no objective existence; they were suggested by Michael Faraday (1791–1867) to give a mental picture of what is happening in the space surrounding a magnet.

6 Electrolysis

I READING AND COMPREHENSION

¹Some liquids which act as conductors of electricity decompose when an electric current is passed through them. ²Such liquids, usually solutions of certain chemicals in water, are known as electrolytes. ³The process by which they are decomposed is called electrolysis.

⁴In electrolysis, two wires or pieces of metal connected to a battery or cell are placed in a vessel containing an electrolyte. ⁵These are called electrodes. ⁶The electrode connected to the negative terminal of the battery (marked '—' in Diagram 1) is called the cathode, and that which is connected to the positive terminal, which is marked '+' in the diagram, is called the anode.

⁷When the current is switched on, it passes from the battery to the anode and then through the electrolyte to the cathode, passing from there back to the battery. ⁸As the current passes from one electrode to the other a chemical reaction takes place.

(a) Liquids which decompose when an electric current passes through them are called electrolytes.
(b) Electrolytes are solutions of certain chemicals in water.
(c) A cathode is an electrode which is connected to the negative terminal of a battery.
(d) A chemical reaction takes place when an electric current passes through an electrolyte.

⁹As an example, let us consider what happens when platinum electrodes are used with an electrolyte of copper sulphate solution. ¹⁰Two pieces of platinum foil are connected to a battery. ¹¹One piece is connected to the positive terminal and the other to the negative. ¹²They are then placed in blue copper sulphate solution contained in a beaker. ¹³A test tube is filled with the

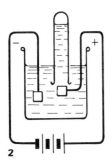

2

solution and fixed over the anode, as shown in Diagram 2. [14]When the current is switched on it passes from the anode to the cathode through the solution. [15]It will be seen that the blue solution of copper sulphate gradually becomes paler as the current passes through it. [16]At the same time, gas is given off from the anode and is collected in the test tube.

[17]The copper sulphate solution gets paler because it is decomposed by the electric current passing through it. [18]It is the copper which gives the solution its blue colour and some of this has been broken up, or dissociated, into electrically charged particles, or ions. [19]When a current passes through the solution, the positively charged ions of copper are attracted to the cathode. [20]There they are neutralized by the negative charge of the cathode and particles of copper are deposited on the platinum foil. [21]Meanwhile, the anode gives off oxygen, which is collected in the test tube.

(e) Gas is given off by the anode as the electric current passes through the solution.

(f) Some of the copper in the copper sulphate solution is broken up into ions when an electric current passes through the solution.

(g) Ions are positively charged particles.

(h) copper deposits form on the cathode.

Solutions

(a) Some liquids which act as conductors of electricity decompose when an electric current is passed through them. (1)
     SUCH LIQUIDS are known as electrolytes. (2)

i.e. The liquids which decompose when an electric current is passed through them are known as electrolytes.
     is passed = passes
     are known as = are called

∴ *Liquids which decompose when an electric current passes through them are called electrolytes.*

(b) Electrolytes are solutions of certain chemicals in water.

= ALL electrolytes are solutions of certain chemicals in water.

= Electrolytes are ALWAYS solutions of certain chemicals in water.

but Such liquids, usually solutions of certain chemicals in water, are known as electrolytes. (2)

i.e. Electrolytes are USUALLY (i.e. not always) solutions of certain chemicals in water.

= MOST (i.e. not all) electrolytes are solutions of certain chemicals in water.

∴ It is NOT TRUE that electrolytes are solutions of certain chemicals in water.

(c) The electrode connected to the negative terminal of a battery is called the cathode. (6)

= The cathode is the electrode connected to the negative terminal of a battery.

= The cathode is the electrode WHICH IS connected to the negative terminal of a battery.

= *A cathode is an electrode which is connected to the negative terminal of a battery.*

(d) As the current passes from one electrode to the other a chemical reaction takes place. (8)

It (i.e. the current) passes to the anode and then through the electrolyte to the cathode. (7)

∴ As the current passes through the electrolyte, a chemical reaction takes place.

= A chemical reaction takes place as the current passes through the electrolyte.

THE ELECTROLYTE refers here to ANY electrolyte.

∴ *A chemical reaction takes place when an electric current passes through an electrolyte.*

(e) The blue solution of copper sulphate gradually becomes paler as the current passes through it. (15)

AT THE SAME TIME gas is given off from the anode. (16)

i.e. *Gas is given off from the anode* AS *the electric current passes through the solution.*

(f) Some of this (i.e. the copper) HAS BEEN broken up into ions. (18)

i.e. It is broken up into ions BEFORE the electric current passes through the solution.

∴ It is NOT TRUE that some of the copper in the copper sulphate solution is broken up into ions when an electric current passes through the solution.

(g) The copper has been broken up into electrically charged particles, or ions. (18)

i.e. Ions are electrically charged particles.

COPPER ions are POSITIVELY charged. (19)

but This does not mean that ALL ions are positively charged.

∴ Ions are NOT (all) positively charged particles.

(h) They (i.e. the ions) are neutralized by the negative charge of the cathode and particles of copper are deposited on the platinum foil. (20)

THE platinum foil = The platinum foil OF THE CATHODE.

∴ Particles of copper are deposited on the platinum foil.

= Particles of copper are deposited on the cathode.

= *Copper deposits form on the cathode.*

EXERCISE A *Contextual reference*

Refer to the context in which the following sentences appear and replace the words in italics with words from the text which make the meaning clear.

EXAMPLE

These are called electrodes. (5)
These wires or pieces of metal are called electrodes.

1. The electrode connected to the negative terminal of the battery is called the cathode, and *that* which is connected to the positive terminal is called the anode. (6)
2. When the current is switched on, it passes from the battery to the anode and then through the electrolyte to the cathode, passing from *there* back to the battery. (7)
3. *They* are then placed in blue copper sulphate solution contained in a beaker. (12)
4. It is the copper which gives the solution its blue colour and some of *this* has been broken up into electrically charged particles. (18)

EXERCISE B *Rephrasing*

Rewrite the following sentences replacing the words printed in italics with expressions which have the same meaning.

1. The electrodes are placed *in a glass jar containing an electrolyte.*
2. The electrode *connected to* the negative terminal *is known as* the cathode (*it is marked '—'* in the diagram).
3. *At the same time* gas is given off from the anode.
4. *The anode gives off oxygen.*
5. It will be seen that the *blue solution of copper sulphate becomes* paler.
6. Some of the copper is *broken up into electrically charged particles.*

EXERCISE C *Labelling diagrams*

Copy Diagrams 1 and 2 on pp. 67 and 68 and label them with reference to the following lists. Draw arrows to indicate the direction of the current.

Diagram 1	*Diagram* 2
battery	platinum foil
electrodes	copper sulphate solution
anode	test tube
cathode	oxygen
electrolyte	copper deposit
switch	anode
vessel	cathode
	beaker
	battery
	+
	—

EXERCISE D *Transformation of directions etc into descriptions*

1. Refer to Problem C, Unit 3 and Problem A, Unit 4, and study the following columns.

I	II
DESCRIPTION	DIRECTIONS
Water is poured into the displacement vessel A until it overflows through the pipe into the measuring jar B. The level of the water surface in the jar is read, and then the solid is lowered into the vessel until it is completely covered by the water. Water is displaced and flows down the pipe into the measuring jar, and the level of the water surface in the jar is read again. The volume of water displaced is equal to the volume of the body.	Pour water into the displacement vessel A until it overflows into the measuring jar B. Read the level of the water surface in the measuring jar. Lower the solid into the vessel until it is completely covered by the water.
	STATEMENT OF RESULT
	Water is displaced and flows down the pipe into the measuring jar.
	DIRECTION
	Read the level of the water surface in the jar again.
	STATEMENT OF RESULT
	The volume of water displaced is equal to the volume of the body.

Change the following descriptions into sets of directions and statements of result as in Column II above.

(a) Two pieces of platinum foil are connected to a battery, one piece to the positive terminal and the other to the negative. The pieces of platinum are then placed in blue copper sulphate solution contained in a beaker. A test tube is filled with the solution and fixed over the anode and the current is then switched on. The copper sulphate solution gradually gets paler as the current passes through it.

(b) Two copper plates are connected to a battery, after having been carefully weighed. They are then placed in a glass vessel containing copper sulphate solution. The current is then switched on. After about half an hour, the current is switched off and the copper plates are taken out of the solution. After they have been dried, they are weighed again. One plate now weighs more than before and the other one weighs less than before, and the weight lost by the one is equal to the weight gained by the other.

(c) A large glass container is half filled with water, and a cork is placed on the surface of the water. A glass is then lowered over the cork and pushed below the water surface. The air in the glass pushes the part of the surface which is under the glass below the surface of the surrounding water.

(d) Two pieces of platinum are connected to a battery and placed in a vessel containing water. When the current is switched on, no reaction takes place.

After a few drops of sulphuric acid are added to the water, however, bubbles of gas begin to form on the electrodes. Those forming on the anode are bubbles of oxygen, and those forming on the cathode are bubbles of hydrogen. (e) Two bar magnets are suspended by separate threads, and the north poles of the two magnets are brought close together. The ends of the two magnets swing away from each other. The north pole of one magnet is then brought close to the south pole of the other. The two poles now attract each other.

2. Compare your answer to (e) above with Exercise D 1(c), Unit 5. *Directions +statements of result* can be changed into *observations* or into *descriptions*.

Change the directions and statements of result in the problems in Unit 1, and in Exercise D 1, Unit 5 into descriptions.

EXAMPLE (Problem A, Unit 1)
A hole is made in the cap of a large plastic water can and the valve from an old bicycle tyre is glued into it. The cap is put back on the can and the can is weighed on a pair of balances. Extra air is then pumped into the can and the can is weighed again. It will be found that the can weighs more after the extra air has been pumped into it than it did before.

NOTE
The same information can be expressed in three different ways:
as a set of directions+statements of result, or as an observation, or as a description.
Which way is chosen depends on the purpose of the writer.
Directions+statements of result are used when the writer wants to give details of how an experiment is to be carried out.
Descriptions are used when the writer wants to describe an experiment as a process.
Observations are used when the writer wants to refer to the results of an experiment in order to make a deduction or induction, or in order to illustrate a generalization.
Each of these ways of expressing information is a different kind of communication.

EXERCISE E *Descriptions of processes*

Combine the following statements to form descriptions of processes.

EXAMPLE
Electrolysis of copper sulphate solution using platinum electrodes.
Two pieces of platinum foil are connected to a battery, one to the positive terminal and one to the negative.
They are placed in a beaker containing blue copper sulphate solution.
A test tube filled with the solution is fixed over the anode.
The current is switched on.

The current passes through the solution from the anode to the cathode.
The solution gradually becomes paler.
Gas is given off from the anode and is collected in the test tube.
Description: sentences 10–16 in the reading passage.

(a) *Electrolysis using copper electrodes*
Two copper plates are weighed.
They are connected to a battery.
They are placed in a vessel containing copper sulphate solution.
The current is switched on.
The current passes from one plate to the other through the copper sulphate solution.
After about half an hour the current is switched off.
The plates are removed from the copper sulphate solution.
They are dried.
They are weighed again.

(b) *Oil refining*
Crude petroleum is placed in a metal vessel, or still.
Steam is passed over the petroleum.
This provides enough heat to change the lightest oils into vapours.
These vapours are carried to a number of pipes surrounded with water, or condensers.
The vapours are cooled and become liquid in the condensers.
The still is heated.
Heavier oils are changed into vapours.
The vapours are led to condensers.
The vapours are liquefied.

(c) *The making of alloys*
The two metals which are the ingredients of the alloy are melted.
The main ingredient is melted.
The other ingredient is melted.
The other ingredient is added to it.
The other ingredient dissolves.
The mixture is poured into metal or sand moulds.
It is allowed to solidify.

(d) *Welding*
The ends of two pieces of metal are carefully cleaned.
They are heated.
The ends become white hot.
A flux is applied to the heated ends.
The flux melts.
The ends are pressed or hammered together.
The joint is smoothed off.

(e) *The preparation of oxygen*
Potassium chlorate crystals are mixed with black manganese (IV) oxide powder.
The mixture is placed in a test tube.
The test tube is fitted with a delivery tube.
The delivery tube leads to a trough of water.
A glass jar containing a column of water is placed upside down in the trough.
The test tube is heated.
The potassium chlorate decomposes.
Oxygen is released.
It passes through the delivery tube.
It is collected in the glass jar.

II PROBLEMS
DIAGRAMS AND DESCRIPTIONS OF PROCESSES

A. Draw and label a diagram of the following process, using the drawings and terms provided.

The preparation of hydrogen
Granules of zinc are placed in a flask. Two glass tubes are fitted into the stopper of the flask. One of these is a thistle funnel. The other is a delivery tube which leads to a trough of water in which is placed an upturned glass jar containing a column of water and supported by a shelf. The end of the delivery tube is placed under the open end of the jar.

Dilute hydrochloric acid is dropped through the thistle funnel on to the granulated zinc. A chemical reaction takes place, and hydrogen is given off. The gas passes through the delivery tube and emerges from the end of the tube as bubbles, which rise through the column of water in the glass jar and displace the water at the top.

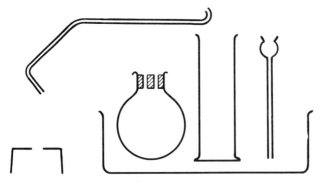

THISTLE FUNNEL
DELIVERY TUBE
FLASK
GLASS JAR
SHELF
TROUGH
DILUTE
    HYDROCHLORIC
    ACID
GRANULES OF ZINC
HYDROGEN

B. Draw a similar diagram of the preparation of oxygen (see Exercise E (e) above).

C. Provide descriptions for the processes which are illustrated by the following diagrams:

(i) The preparation of ....

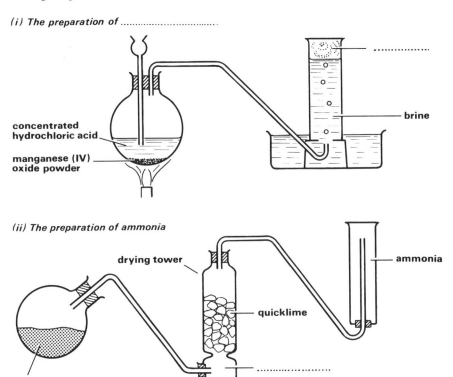

concentrated hydrochloric acid

manganese (IV) oxide powder

brine

(ii) The preparation of ammonia

drying tower

quicklime

ammonia

....

III GRAMMAR

EXERCISE A *The use of time expressions*

Look at the following sentence:
1. *First* [**A.** the air leaves the compressor] *then* [**B.** it enters the combustion chambers].
The sequence *first* [**A**] *then* [**B**] can also be expressed as follows:
2. *After* [**A.** the air leaves the compressor] [**B.** it enters the combustion chambers].
First [**A**] then [**B**] = After [**A**][**B**]

(i) Rewrite the sentences below by selecting one of the time expressions given in brackets and putting it at the beginning of the sentence. Select the time expression which is closest in meaning to the words in italics. These words are then omitted.

EXAMPLE
First the air leaves the compressor *then* it enters the combustion chambers. (after, until)
After the air leaves the compressor it enters the combustion chambers.

1. the water vapour condenses to water *as a result* it is able to fall downwards as rain or snow (when, before)
2. the water reaches the town supply *but first* it is purified by filtering through gravel beds (before, after)
3. the body is immersed in the fluid *then* the upthrust is found to be equal to the weight of the fluid displaced (before, after)
4. the aluminium is in the measuring cylinder *during this time* we may measure the volume of water displaced (as soon as, while)
5. *first* the water is forced out of the ballast tanks by compressed air *before this* the submarine is not able to rise to the surface (until, when)
6. the balloon ascends *after some time* it reaches regions of lower pressure and the gas inside expands (before, as)
7. a vacuum forms *immediately* water from the beaker rushes up and fills the flask (after, as soon as)
8. we will carry out this experiment *but first* it is necessary to examine the nature of the changes involved (before, as soon as)
9. the air is heated *immediately* it expands and becomes less dense, so that it floats upwards, making an air current and carrying its heat energy with it (until, as soon as)
10. the water evaporates *as a result* it turns from visible liquid to invisible water vapour and the vapour exerts a pressure on the surface of the mercury, pushing it down (when, until)
11. the water is boiling *during this process* close the flask firmly with a rubber bung and remove the flask from the flame (after, while)
12. the reaction has taken place *now* the apparatus is again weighed, but no change in weight is recorded (while, after)

(ii) Compare the following sentences with your answers to Exercise A (i). If the sentences have approximately the same meaning, write 'same'; if not, write 'different'. The first two sentences have been done for you.

1. Water vapour falls as rain or snow but the vapour must condense to water first. (same)
2. The water reaches the town supply, then it is purified. (different)
3. We cannot measure the upthrust until the body is immersed in the fluid.
4. A volume of water is displaced and as a result we can put the aluminium in the measuring cylinder.
5. A submarine is not able to rise to the surface while the ballast tanks are full of water.

6. The gas expands and as a result the balloon ascends.

7. A vacuum is formed, then water enters the flask after a short delay.

8. First we will carry out the experiment, then we will examine the nature of the changes involved.

9. When the air is heated it expands and becomes less dense straight away.

10. (a) the water evaporates; (b) it turns into invisible water vapour; (a) causes (b).

11. First we close the flask, then the water boils.

12. First the reaction takes place, then the apparatus is weighed.

EXERCISE B *Short-form time clauses*

Look at these sentences:

Before [the effluent] reaches the river, [it] ⎱ passes through a cleansing
Before [it] reaches the river, [the effluent] ⎰ plant.

These time clauses may be shortened as follows:

Before reaching the river, the effluent passes through a cleansing plant.

Note the following:
Before/Prior to reaching the domestic supply, the current passes through a fuse box.
When/While/In passing through a nozzle, the liquid is reduced to a fine spray.
After/On leaving the heart, the blood circulates again through the body.

Rewrite the sentences, changing each time statement into an appropriate short form.

1. While we are producing chlorine gas we should take a number of precautions.

2. Before the hydrogen reaches the jet, it passes through a u-tube containing calcium chloride.

3. After they lose their charges the copper ions become copper atoms, which stick to the cathode.

4. While they are passing through very cold air on their way to the earth, the raindrops may become frozen, forming hail.

5. After the steam escapes from the cylinder, it expands very considerably.

6. Before the tinstone is smelted with coke or charcoal, it requires considerable treatment.

7. When the food passes through the alimentary canal, it undergoes a series of treatments.

8. After they return to the ground, the compounds and elements become available to be used again in building up new forms of life.

9. While the gas passes upwards through the red-hot coke, it is reduced to carbon monoxide.

10. Before they build a bridge or any stress-bearing structure, the designers must carefully calculate the stresses which they expect the structure to bear.

IV   PARAGRAPH WRITING

STAGE 1 *Sentence building*

Join each of the fifteen groups of words below into one sentence, using the additional material at the beginning of each group. Omit words in italics. Number your sentences and begin each one with a capital letter.

1   THE TERMINALS OF/AND/AND
    connect wires to a flash-lamp bulb
    connect a zinc plate to one wire
    connect a copper plate to the other *wire*

2   OF HYDROGEN/COPPER/AND/,/SHOWING THAT/IT
    bubbles will rise from the plate
    the bulb will glow
    a current is passing through *the bulb*

3   THAT/,/BECOMING/, AND/FROM THE SOLUTION/ITS
    some hydrogen ions *are* in contact with the copper plate
    these hydrogen ions take up electrons
    the electrons are flowing to *the copper* plate
    the hydrogen ions become hydrogen atoms
    the removal of hydrogen ions reduces *the* positive potential

4   THE/POSITIVE/AND/NEGATIVE
    sulphuric acid contains hydrogen ions
    sulphuric acid contains 'sulphate' ions

5   THAT/AN ELECTRIC
    we say *this*
    a current passes through the wire

6   IF/DILUTE/AND/IT/,/THERE IS
    we put some sulphuric acid in a beaker
    we dip a plate of pure zinc in *the sulphuric acid*
    no visible action *occurs*

7   DILUTE/BUT/THEM
    dip the plates into sulphuric acid
    do not allow *the plates* to touch

8   IF/PLATES/ONE ANOTHER/OR/,/WHICH
    the copper *plate* and *the* zinc *plate* touch
    the two plates are connected by a conductor
    excess electrons flow from the zinc plate to the copper plate
    the copper plate is at a higher potential

9   AND A PLATE OF ZINC/DIPPING/FORM OF/, AND/THE/TAKING
    a plate of copper *dips* into sulphuric acid
    this constitutes a simple electric cell
    an action *takes* place in it
    this action may be described as follows

10 POSITIVE/INTO THE SOLUTION/ZINC/AND
    more ions can escape from the plate
    the process becomes continuous

11 ZINC/BEHIND/ZINC/,/WHICH/NEGATIVELY/
    IN CONSEQUENCE
    each ion leaves two electrons on the plate
    the zinc plate becomes charged

12 IF/BY A WIRE/FROM THE ZINC PLATE/THROUGH THE WIRE
    the two plates are connected
    the electrons flow to the copper plate

13 IF/, BUT/WITHOUT ALLOWING/IT/,/STILL/WILL BE OBSERVED
    we dip a plate of copper into the acid
    we do not allow the copper plate to touch the zinc plate
    no *visible* action *occurs*

14 THERE IS A TENDENCY FOR/AND/FOR/TO
    the zinc *tends* to dissolve
    zinc ions pass into the solution

15 IF/PLATES/ONE ANOTHER,/AT ONCE/COPPER
    we allow the zinc *plate* and *the* copper *plate* to touch
    bubbles of hydrogen will rise from the plate

STAGE 2 *Paragraph building*

Rewrite the fifteen sentences in a logical order to make a paragraph. Before
you write the paragraph, add the following material:
    write 'now' at the beginning of sentence 1
    write 'in this case' at the beginning of sentence 5
    write 'as a result' at the beginning of sentence 10
    write 'when this happens' at the beginning of sentence 11
    write 'however,' at the beginning of sentence 15.
When you have written your paragraph re-read it and make sure that the
sentences are presented in a logical order. Give the paragraph a suitable title.

Compare your paragraph with the relevant paragraph in the Free Reading passage. Make any changes that you think are necessary, but remember that sentences can often be arranged in more than one way.

STAGE 3 *Paragraph reconstruction*

Read through the paragraph again. Make sure you know all the words, using a dictionary if necessary. Without referring to your previous work rewrite the paragraph. Here are some notes to help you.

sulphuric acid – beaker – plate of zinc – no action
plate of copper – without touching zinc – no action
zinc and copper touch – bubbles from copper plate
connect wires – flash-lamp bulb – connect zinc plate – copper plate
dip plates into acid – do not allow to touch
bubbles from copper plate – bulb will glow – current passing
simple electric cell – action as follows
sulphuric acid – positive ions – negative ions
zinc dissolves – zinc ions pass into solution
two electrons on zinc plate – negatively charged
copper and zinc plates touch – connected by conductor – excess electrons
    flow – higher potential
more positive ions escape – process continuous
two plates – connected by wire – electrons flow
electric current – through wire

V   FREE READING

Read the following passage in your own time. Try to find additional examples of the points you have studied in this and other Units.

We have seen that some liquids act as conductors of electricity and decompose when an electric current is passed through them. Such liquids are called electrolytes and the process by which they are decomposed is known as electrolysis. Acids, alkalis and salts are the main classes of compounds which behave as electrolytes. When such substances are dissolved in water some of their molecules break up into ions. For example, when sodium chloride is dissolved in water the sodium and chlorine atoms separate, each chlorine atom taking with it one of the electrons from a sodium atom. As a result positively charged sodium ions and negatively charged chlorine ions are produced in the solution, as indicated by the following equation:

$$NaCl = Na^+ + Cl^-$$

Generally speaking, metal atoms and hydrogen atoms from acids become positive ions, while atoms and groups of atoms of non-metals form negative ions.

Electrolysis was first investigated by Michael Faraday, who investigated the relation between the quantity of electricity passing through an electrolyte and the quantity of substance liberated by it. The results of Faraday's experiments are summed up in two laws which are known as Faraday's laws of electrolysis:

(1) The weight of a substance liberated at an electrode is proportional to the quantity of electricity which has passed through the electrolyte.

(2) When the same quantity of electricity is passed through different electrolytes, the weights of substances liberated are in the ratio of their chemical equivalent weights.

The equivalent weight of an element is the weight that combines with or displaces 1 g of hydrogen. Thus, if the equivalent weight of oxygen is 8 and of silver 107·9, the same quantity of electricity which liberates 1 g of hydrogen will liberate 8 g of oxygen and 107·9 g of silver.

If we put some dilute sulphuric acid in a beaker and dip a plate of pure zinc in it, there is no visible action. If we dip a plate of copper into the acid, but without allowing it to touch the zinc plate, still no action will be observed. However, if we allow the zinc and copper plates to touch one another, at once bubbles of hydrogen will rise from the copper plate. Now connect wires to the terminals of a flash-lamp bulb and connect a zinc plate to one wire and a copper plate to the other. Dip the plates into dilute sulphuric acid but do not allow them to touch. Bubbles of hydrogen will rise from the copper plate and the bulb will glow, showing that a current is passing through it. A plate of copper and a plate of zinc dipping into sulphuric acid constitutes a simple form of electric cell, and the action taking place in it may be described as follows. The sulphuric acid contains positive hydrogen ions and negative 'sulphate' ions. There is a tendency for the zinc to dissolve, and for zinc ions to pass into the solution. When this happens each zinc ion leaves two electrons behind on the zinc plate, which becomes negatively charged in consequence. If the copper and zinc plates touch one another or are connected by a conductor excess electrons flow from the zinc plate to the copper plate, which is at a higher potential. Hydrogen ions in contact with the copper plate take up electrons flowing to that plate, becoming hydrogen atoms, and the removal of hydrogen ions from the solution reduces its positive potential. As a result more positive ions can escape into the solution from the zinc plate and the process becomes continuous. If the two plates are connected by a wire the electrons flow from the zinc plate to the copper plate through the wire. In this case we say that an electric current passes through the wire.

7 The Electric Bell

I READING AND COMPREHENSION

PASSAGE A *The components of the bell*

An electric bell operates by means of an electromagnet. This consists of two cylinders of soft iron fixed one above the other to a soft iron bar. Around these cylinders is wound a length of copper wire, the direction of winding being reversed as the wire passes from one cylinder to the other. One end of it passes from the free end of the upper cylinder and is connected to a battery terminal. The other end passes down from the top of the lower cylinder and is connected to the fixed end of a steel spring which is situated below and to the left of the electromagnet. To the right side of this spring is attached a metal rod, the head of which acts as a hammer, or striker. The spring passes up the left side of the striker rod and then bends outwards to touch a screw, or key, which is connected to the other terminal of the battery by means of copper wire. On the other side of the striker rod, just opposite the free ends of the soft iron cylinders, is fixed a piece of soft iron which is called the armature. Above the electromagnet, and close to the head of the striker rod, is a gong.

EXERCISE A *Composition of a diagram based on a description*

Make a diagram of an electric bell, as described in the passage by putting together the parts illustrated below. Use a different coloured pen or pencil to draw in the copper wire.

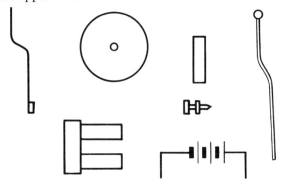

Label the diagram you have drawn with the following terms:

   SOFT IRON CYLINDERS / SOFT IRON BAR / BATTERY / KEY / GONG /
   STEEL SPRING / STRIKER ROD / ARMATURE

Indicate with arrows how the wire is wound on the two cylinders.

EXERCISE B *Statements about diagrams*

1. Make statements about the position of A relative to B in the following diagrams by using the given expressions.

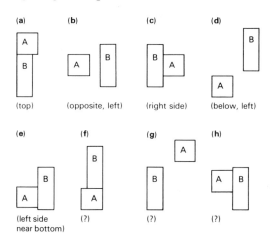

EXAMPLES

   Diagram (a) – A is attached (*or* fixed) to the top of B.
   Diagram (b) – A is opposite and to the left of B.

2. Make statements about the way in which A is connected to B in the following diagrams by using the given expressions. The line between the boxes represents a piece (or length) of copper wire.

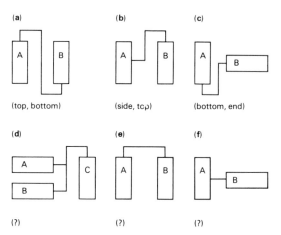

EXAMPLE

Diagram (a) – A piece (*or* length) of copper wire passes from the top of A to the bottom of B.

OR The top of A is connected to the bottom of B by means of a length of copper wire.

PASSAGE B *The operation of the bell*

To operate the bell, the key, or screw, is connected to the positive terminal of the battery, and the copper wire coming from the electromagnet is connected to the negative terminal. When the current is switched on, it flows through the key into the spring, passing from there round the coils of the electromagnet and then back to the battery. As the current passes through the coils of copper wire, the soft iron cylinders around which it is wound become magnetized. Consequently, they attract the armature, causing the head of the striker rod to hit the gong. As the striker hits the gong, the spring to which it is fixed loses contact with the screw, breaking the circuit. The current ceasing to flow, the electromagnet loses its magnetism and the armature, being no longer attracted, is pulled back by the spring. When this happens, the spring makes contact with the screw once more, allowing the electric current to pass, again magnetizing the cylinders. These then attract the armature, once more pulling the spring away from the screw and breaking the circuit. The whole process is repeated over and over again, causing the head of the striker to vibrate rapidly against the gong, thus producing the familiar sound of an electric bell.

EXERCISE A *Illustrating the reading passage with diagrams*

Illustrate the above text by drawing two diagrams: one showing the positions of the parts of the bell when the circuit is complete, and one showing their positions when the circuit is broken.

Label the diagrams which you have drawn and shade in the parts of the bell which move.

EXERCISE B *Description of a sequence of events*

(i) Put the expressions *after, before, when* in the blank spaces so as to make statements which are correct according to the passage.

1. The current passes into the spring . . . it passes through the key.
2. The current passes into the battery . . . it passes through the coils of copper wire.
3. The soft iron cylinders are magnetized . . . the current passes through the coils of copper wire.
4. The spring makes contact with the key . . . the electromagnet loses its magnetism.

5. The spring is pulled away from the key . . . the head of the striker hits the gong.

6. The armature is pulled back by the spring . . . the spring makes contact with the screw.

7. The striker hits the gong . . . the electromagnet loses its magnetism.

8. The electromagnet loses its magnetism . . . the striker hits the gong.

(ii) Refer to Grammar Exercise A in Unit 6. Change the statements you have made above by using sentences of the following form.

First [A] then [B]   After/Before/When [A] [B]

EXAMPLE

First the current passes through the key (and) then (it passes) into the spring.

or:

The current *first* passes through the key (and) then (it passes) into the spring.

After the current passes through the key, it passes into the spring.

or:

Before the current passes into the spring, it passes through the key.

The soft iron cylinders are magnetized *when* the current passes through the coils of copper wire.

or:

The current passes through the coils of copper wire *when* the soft iron cylinders are magnetized.

(iii) Refer to Grammar Exercise B in Unit 6 to guide you. Change the statements you have just made by using short-form time clauses where possible.

EXAMPLE

After passing through the key, the current passes into the spring.

II PROBLEMS
DIAGRAMS AND DESCRIPTIONS OF DEVICES

A. Illustrate the following descriptions with diagrams according to the instructions given in each case.

(i) *The mercury thermometer*

Thermometers are instruments which are used to measure temperature. The most common thermometer consists of a tube with a very narrow bore, known as a capillary tube, which is sealed at one end. At the other end of the tube there is a bulb containing mercury. When the thermometer is made, the air between the sealed end of the tube and the level of mercury in the bulb is removed, creating a vacuum. The tube is marked with a measuring scale by reference to two fixed points; the lower fixed point, which is the temperature at which ice melts, and the upper fixed point, which is the temperature at which pure water boils under normal atmospheric pressure. The space between the two points may be marked out on two different scales: the Celsius scale, on which the fixed points are 0°C and 100°C, or the Fahrenheit scale, on which the fixed points are 32°F and 212°F.

Draw a diagram of a thermometer and label it with the following terms:
CAPILLARY TUBE / BULB / VACUUM / MERCURY / LOWER FIXED POINT /
UPPER FIXED POINT / MEASURING SCALE
Mark in the degrees of the fixed points on the Celsius scale on one side of the tube, and the degrees of the fixed points on the Fahrenheit scale on the other.

(ii) *The aneroid barometer*
Barometers are instruments which are used for measuring atmospheric pressure. The aneroid barometer consists of a thin metal box in the shape of a concertina containing a partial vacuum. The box is prevented from collapsing by means of a steel spring fixed at the side of it. This spring is bent over the top of the box, exerting pressure upon it by means of a metal shaft, one end of which is attached to the spring. The other end is attached to a flat piece of metal which presses down on the top of the box. The spring extends sideways from the top of the metal shaft and then bends downwards to connect up with a short horizontal lever which is connected to a long vertical lever by means of a pivot. The longer lever extends upwards and is connected to a thread which passes sideways and winds on to the axle of a pointer fixed above a dial. A small coiled spring is attached to this axle.

Make a diagram of an aneroid barometer as described in this text by putting together the parts illustrated below.

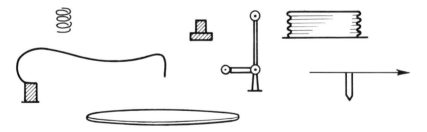

Label your diagram with the following terms:
SPRING / PIVOT / COILED SPRING / SHAFT / METAL BOX / PARTIAL
VACUUM / DIAL / AXLE / LEVERS / POINTER / THREAD

Describe how an aneroid barometer works. Refer to Passage B and use as many of the following expressions as you find necessary:

atmospheric pressure	axle	attach
metal shaft	pointer	turn
short horizontal lever	dial	upwards
long vertical lever	decrease	at
spring	pull (verb)	over
pull (noun)	push	the top of
thread	cause	to the right
coiled spring	move	

B. Write descriptions of a water pump by referring to the diagrams provided. First describe the parts, or components, of the pump (see Passage A). Then describe the way it works, beginning

'On the upstroke, when the handle is pulled down, the piston valve closes. . . .' (see Passage B)

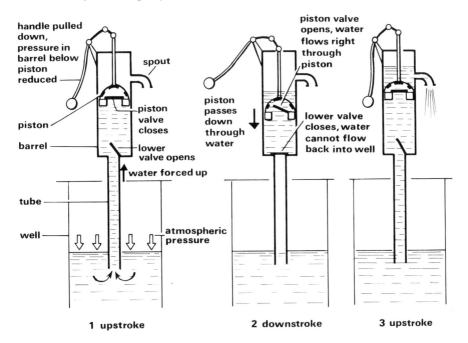

III GRAMMAR

EXERCISE A *The use of the -ing form*

An *ing*-clause can be used

(i) as a *simple addition* to a preceding statement:
   We keep the solution hot and add further small quantities of the oxide, *letting each dissolve before the next is added.*

(ii) as an *explanation*:

The molten iron, *having been in contact with coke in the lower part of the furnace*, contains several percent of dissolved carbon.

(iii) to show a *result* or *consequence*:

Nitric acid will dissolve nearly all the common metals, *forming their nitrates*.

If the subject of the *ing*-clause is the same as the subject of the main clause it is omitted, as in the above examples. However, if the two subjects are different the subject of the *ing*-clause must be stated:

The atom and its sub-units are so small that an ordinary microscope is no longer of help, *light itself not being a delicate enough probe*.

Combine each pair of statements into a sentence containing an *ing*-clause. State whether the *ing*-clause is an addition, an explanation, or a result.

EXAMPLE

Earthworms tunnel through the soil. Earthworms cause excellent aeration.
= Earthworms tunnel through the soil causing excellent aeration.   (result)

1. The zeolite is able to remove the ions from the water. The zeolite replaces them by the sodium ion.
2. The salt dissolves in water. The salt makes a solution which is in equilibrium with ice at a temperature below the freezing point of water.
3. At the end of the process a solution of ammonium chloride remains. The sodium hydrogen carbonate has been precipitated out.
4. In these reactions the hydrated ions of aluminium lose protons. The hydrated ions of aluminium form successive hydroxide complexes.
5. If an aircraft is standing on the ground the air pressure on all its different parts is the same. Air pressure is exerted equally in all directions.
6. A solute such as alcohol or glycerol added to the radiator water keeps the water from freezing. The freezing point of a solution is lower than that of the pure solvent.
7. Quite possibly larger amounts of carbon dioxide existed in the atmosphere during the Carboniferous Period than at the present time. Larger amounts of carbon dioxide permitted plant life to flourish and the great coal beds to be laid down.
8. Carbon is the first element of the fourth group of the periodic table. The others are silicon, germanium, tin and lead.
9. Sulphuric acid must be considered one of the most important of all chemicals. Sulphuric acid is used throughout the chemical industry and related industries.
10. White phosphorus ignites at about 35°C and oxidizes slowly at room temperature. The white phosphorus gives off a white light.

11. The metallic solutions slowly decompose, with evolution of hydrogen. The metallic solutions form amides, such as sodamide, $NaNH_2$.

12. Stable molecules and complex ions usually have structures such that each atom has the electronic structure of a noble-gas atom. The shared electrons of each covalent bond are counted for each of the two atoms connected by the covalent bond.

EXERCISE B *Patterns expressing result*

A number of patterns can be used to express result:

The electric field is turned on, *so that* the plates are charged.
The electric field is turned on, *with the result that* the plates are charged.
The electric field is turned on. *As a result* the plates are charged.

Combine each pair of statements, using one of the above patterns.

1. The electrodes are then put into the solution. The sodium ions are attracted towards the cathode, and the chloride ions are attracted towards the anode.

2. The mixture of aluminium powder and iron (III) oxide, Fe_2O_3, is ignited. The reaction $2Al+Fe_2O_3 = 2Fe+Al_2O_3$ takes place

3. Sulphur dioxide destroys fungi and bacteria. It can be used as a preservative in the preparation of dried fruits.

4. The rate of the reaction is very slow at low temperatures. The direct combination of the substances is unsuitable as a commercial process.

5. Sulphuric acid has a high boiling point. It can be used with salts of more volatile acids in the preparation of these acids.

6. The arrangement of the framework of tetrahedra in the glass is irregular. A very small region may resemble quartz and an adjacent region may resemble cristobalite.

7. Manganese steel is extraordinarily hard. It can be used to make crushing and grinding machines and safes.

8. Iron becomes passive when it is dipped in very concentrated nitric acid. It no longer displaces hydrogen from dilute acids.

9. The silver halogenides are sensitive to light. They undergo photochemical decomposition.

10. Atoms are not hard spheres. By increased force they may be pushed more closely together.

IV PARAGRAPH WRITING

STAGE 1 *Sentence building*

Join each of the thirteen groups of words below into one sentence, using the additional material at the beginning of each group. Omit words in italics. Number your sentences and begin each one with a capital letter.

1   ARE SAID/TO BE/,/WHILE/AND PIECES OF IRON OR GLASS,/WHICH/
    THEMSELVES/,/ARE SAID/TO BE
    we say that such bodies *are* luminous
    bodies such as bricks do not produce light
    we say that these bodies are non-luminous

2   THREADED/THAT/THEY
    thread a length of cotton through the holes
    this will demonstrate *this*
    the holes are in a straight line

3   THAT/,/A/WHICH/MEANS OF/THE FOLLOWING
    these observations suggest *this*
    light travels in straight lines
    this fact can be verified by *an* experiment

4   SUCH AS CLEAR GLASS AND WATER/WHICH/SO THAT/CAN BE/SEEN/
    ARE SAID/TO BE
    some substances allow light to pass through them
    we can see objects on the other side clearly
    we say that these substances are transparent

5   AND/SMALL/THE MIDDLE OF/OF THEM
    take three pieces of cardboard
    make a hole in each *piece*

6   MOST/WHICH/,/FOR/,/GLOWING/AN ELECTRIC/,/OR
    some bodies emit light
    some bodies also emit heat
    one example *is* the sun
    another example is the filament of *a* light bulb
    another example is a fire

7   FROM A POCKET TORCH, A SEARCHLIGHT OR CAR HEADLAMPS/
    , AND/UNLESS/DO SO/THE HELP OF/OR SOME OTHER REFLECTING
    DEVICE
    a beam of light appears to have straight edges
    a beam of light will not bend round corners
    a beam of light is made to *bend* with mirrors

8   ALL/LIGHT/AND/THAT
    these bodies emit energy
    they can be seen by the light
    they give out *light*

9   WHICH/WITHOUT/BEING/ARE SAID/TO BE/, WHILE/WHICH/THE
    PASSAGE OF/ARE SAID/TO BE
    some substances allow light to pass through them
    objects on the other side *are not* clearly seen

we say that these substances are translucent
some substances do not permit light *to pass*
we say that these substances are opaque

10 IF/IS MOVED/SO THAT/NO LONGER/,
   move one of the pieces of cardboard slightly
   the holes are *not* in a straight line
   the light will be cut off

11 ,/LIKE/,/, AND/THERE IS/THE TWO
   light *is a form of energy*
   heat is a form of energy
   a close connection *exists* between *light and heat*

12 LIGHT/BUT/WHEN/FROM LUMINOUS BODIES/AND/FROM THEIR
   SURFACES
   non-luminous bodies do not emit energy
   they can be seen
   light falls on them
   light is reflected

13 PIECES OF/SO THAT/FROM A CANDLE FLAME/CAN BE SEEN/THREE/
   AT THE SAME TIME
   arrange the cardboard
   we can see the light through all *the* holes

STAGE 2 *Paragraph building*

Rewrite the thirteen sentences in a logical order to make two paragraphs.
The first paragraph should contain a number of definitions, and the second
paragraph should deal with the fact that light travels in straight lines. Before
you write the paragraphs, add the following material:
   write 'this is shown by the fact that' at the beginning of sentence 6.
   When you have written your paragraphs, re-read them and make sure that
the sentences are presented in a logical order. Compare your paragraphs
with the relevant paragraphs in the Free Reading passage. Make any changes
that you think are necessary, but remember that sentences can often be
arranged in more than one way.

STAGE 3: *Paragraph reconstruction*

Read through the paragraphs again. Make sure you know all the words,
using a dictionary if necessary. Without referring to your previous work rewrite the paragraphs. Here are some notes to help you.
paragraph 1
   light – heat – forms of energy – close connection
   emit heat and light: sun, light bulb, fire
   these bodies emit light energy – can be seen by light given out

luminous, non-luminous bodies
non-luminous bodies – no light energy – can be seen – reflected light
transparent substances
translucent, opaque substances
paragraph 2
beam of light – straight edges – will not bend
light travels in straight lines – experiment
three pieces of cardboard – small hole
light from candle flame
length of cotton
move one piece of cardboard slightly

V   FREE READING

Read the following passage in your own time. Try to find additional examples of the points you have studied in this and other Units.

Light, like heat, is a form of energy, and there is a close connection between the two. This is shown by the fact that most bodies which emit light also emit heat, for example the sun, the glowing filament of an electric light bulb, or a fire. All these bodies emit light energy and can be seen by the light that they give out. Such bodies are said to be luminous, while bodies such as bricks and pieces of iron or glass, which do not themselves produce light, are said to be non-luminous. Non-luminous bodies do not emit light energy but they can be seen when light from luminous bodies falls on them and is reflected from their surfaces. Substances such as clear glass and water which allow light to pass through them so that objects on the other side can be clearly seen are said to be transparent. Substances which allow light to pass through them without objects on the other side being clearly seen are said to be translucent, while substances which do not permit the passage of light are said to be opaque.

A beam of light from a pocket torch, a searchlight or car headlamps appears to have straight edges, and will not bend round corners unless made to do so with the help of mirrors or some other reflecting device. These observations suggest that light travels in straight lines, a fact which can be verified by means of the following experiment. Take three pieces of cardboard and make a small hole in the middle of each of them. Arrange the pieces of cardboard so that light from a candle flame can be seen through all three holes at the same time. A length of cotton threaded through the holes will demonstrate that they are in a straight line. If one of the pieces of cardboard is moved slightly so that the holes are no longer in a straight line, the light will be cut off.

The formation of shadows is a result of the fact that light travels in straight lines. If an opaque object is placed in front of a small source of light, such as a pocket torch, the light will throw a sharp shadow of the object on to a screen. The shadow will have the same shape as the object, but it will be larger than the object. Diagram 1 explains why this is so:

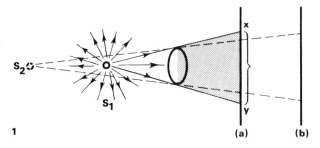

1   (a)   (b)

Light spreads out along straight lines in all directions around the small source, S_1, but that light which falls on the opaque object is stopped. The light which passes the edges of the object cannot bend round it, with the result that there is a clear-cut dark space behind the object. A shadow of the object will appear on a screen placed in position (a) since a section of the screen having the same shape as the object will receive no light. If the source is moved further from the object, to S_2, the shadow will become smaller, and if the screen is moved back to (b) the shadow will become larger.

Let us suppose now that we use a larger source of light. We will notice that the shadow obtained has a perfectly dark centre portion surrounded by a region that is only partly darkened. The formation of such shadows is illustrated in Diagram 2. A lamp is put inside a box which has a hole covered by tissue paper in one of its sides, and an opaque object is placed between the box and a screen. The area xq will not receive light from any part of ab and will therefore be perfectly dark. The area px will receive light from the upper part of ab but not from the lower part with the result that px will be partly darkened. Similarly, the area qy will receive light from the lower part of ab but not from the upper part, so that qy also will be partly darkened. All that area of the screen which falls outside pq will be fully lighted by all parts of ab. The dark part of the shadow is called the umbra, and the partly darkened portion the penumbra.

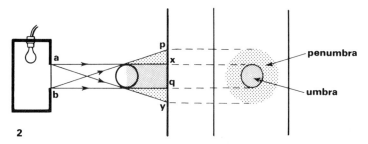

2

8 Summary and Extension Exercises

I COMPREHENSION QUESTIONS

Write out answers to the following comprehension questions, based on the passages in the Free Reading sections of the units mentioned.

UNIT 1

(a) Why does an inner tube weigh less when it is deflated than when it is inflated?
(b) Why do we not feel the weight of the atmosphere?
(c) What happens when a tin can containing a little water is heated?
(d) What happens to the air in the can?
(e) Why is the pressure in the can less when the can cools down?

UNIT 2

(a) What does a molecule of water consist of?
(b) What is a compound?
(c) What is an element?
(d) What are the characteristics of acids?
(e) Why are alkalis frequently used for cleaning?
(f) What is the difference between a base and a salt?
(g) What happens if a solution of sodium hydroxide is added to a beaker containing hydrochloric acid and red litmus?
(h) What is shown by litmus changing from red to blue?
(i) What happens when hydrochloric acid is neutralized by sodium hydroxide?

UNIT 3

(a) What happens when a stone is suspended from a spring balance and gradually lowered into water?
(b) What happens when the stone is withdrawn from the water?

(c) What was the principle stated by Archimedes?

(d) How do we find the volume of an irregular solid?

(e) A piece of metal is weighed in air and in water. Weight of metal in air = 20·23 g; apparent weight of metal in water = 17·34 g. What is the relative density of the metal?

(f) A piece of metal is weighed in air, in water and in paraffin. Weight of metal in air = 20·23 g; apparent weight of metal in water = 17·34 g; apparent weight of metal in paraffin = 17·92 g. What is the relative density of paraffin.

(g) What is the law of flotation?

(h) What objects do we need in order to set up an experiment to verify the law of flotation?

UNIT 4

(a) What happens when we bore holes at different levels in the sides of a can and fill the can with water?

(b) What does this show?

(c) How is pressure utilized in a domestic water system?

(d) Why are reservoirs usually located on high ground?

(e) Why are artesian wells so called?

(f) Look at Diagram 1. Would an artesian well work if A and C consisted of porous rock? Why not?

(g) What is a hydraulic press and what is it used for?

UNIT 5

(a) What is a natural magnet?

(b) Why was magnetite used as a compass?

(c) What are the poles of a magnet?

(d) How can we demonstrate that a bar-magnet has poles?

(e) What happens when we float a bar-magnet on a cork? What does this show?

(f) 'Like poles repel, unlike poles attract.' What does this mean?

(g) What is a magnetic field?

(h) What is a line of magnetic force?

(i) 'Lines of force have no objective existence and therefore there is no point in talking about them.' Do you agree?

(j) Draw a labelled diagram to illustrate the experiment described in the third paragraph.

UNIT 6

(a) What is an electrolyte?

(b) What is electrolysis?

(c) Describe the process indicated by the equation $NaCl = Na^+ + Cl^-$.

(d) What did Faraday discover when he investigated the relation between the quantity of electricity passing through an electrolyte and the quantity of substance liberated by it?

(e) Draw a diagram to illustrate what happens when a zinc plate and a copper plate are connected by wires to a bulb and dipped into dilute sulphuric acid. Label the diagram.

(f) How does the zinc plate become negatively charged?

(g) What happens when hydrogen ions are removed from the solution?

(h) What do we mean when we say that an electric current passes through the wire?

UNIT 7

(a) What is a luminous body?

(b) What is a non-luminous body?

(c) What is a transparent substance?

(d) What is a translucent substance?

(e) What is an opaque substance?

(f) How do we know that light travels in straight lines?

(g) Explain how shadows are formed.

(h) Why is it that the shadow in Diagram 1 does not have a penumbra as in Diagram 2?

II WORD STUDY

EXERCISE A *Adjectives formed from nouns and verbs*

Many adjectives are formed from nouns and verbs by adding various suffixes. Draw the following table and complete it, using your dictionary if necessary. (In this exercise avoid using participles ending in *-ed* or *-ing*)

Noun	Verb	Adjective
atmosphere		atmospheric
	continue	
	vibrate	
molecule		
sphere		
	move	
osmosis		
gas		
	progress	
rectangle		
	emerge	
result		
chemistry		
friction		
	explode	
nitrogen		
microscope		

Write out the following sentences, substituting an adjective from the above table for each of the blank spaces:

1. The fuel in a steam engine is burnt in the furnace, and it forms hot ... products which convey their heat by conduction and convection to the water in the boiler.
2. When a small drop of mercury falls on to a surface it invariably takes up a ... shape.
3. To get a ... stream of water the pump has to be modified by including a dome-shaped vessel containing air.
4. Some plants live on peaty soil from which they cannot get much ... food.
5. Pressure is required to force the liquid up the tube, and this is called ... pressure.
6. Many ... substances can be formed by the action of nitric acid on the so-called organic compounds.
7. The magnetic field at the ends of the bar is increased and the field at the sides is decreased; the ... field due to the original field and the bar is represented in the diagram.
8. The molecules of a substance are believed to have a ... motion which is responsible for the heat energy in the substance.
9. The art of cutting a diamond is to produce surfaces so that the light is emitted only in certain directions; hence the ... light is very brilliant and the stone sparkles.
10. ... examination of the gills of a mushroom shows a large number of spore cases growing from their sides.
11. Changes in which new substances quite distinct in their properties from the original substances are formed, are called ... changes.
12. A wave which continues without interruption, and in which each particle of the medium in turn goes through a similar movement, is called a ... wave.
13. Beyond a certain distance, called the range of ... attraction, the attraction of a molecule on a neighbouring one is inappreciable.
14. The viscosity of a liquid is explained by the ... forces existing between various layers.
15. When we consider the mechanical advantage of a ... pulley, we must remember that the total load to be raised by the effort is the actual load on the pulley together with the weight of the pulley block itself.
16. Below the epidermis on the upper surface of a leaf is a layer of long ... cells known as the palisade layer.

EXERCISE B *Nouns formed from verbs and adjectives*

Many abstract nouns used in scientific writing are formed from verbs and adjectives. Draw and complete the following table. You may write more than one noun in each box, but avoid using participles ending in *-ing*.

Adjective	Verb	Noun
	evaporate	evaporation
	adjust	
	rotate	
	disinfect	
	weigh	
ductile		
	press	
solid		
	retain	
	displace	
	relate	
dense		
	manufacture	
deep		

Write out the following sentences, substituting an abstract noun from the above table for each of the blank spaces:

1. Metals are a class of chemical elements which are characterized by . . ., malleability, lustre and conductivity.

2. Let us consider an example of a process which illustrates the . . . between acids, bases and salts.

3. Relative . . . is equal to the . . . of the solid divided by the . . . of the same volume of water.

4. We can change a . . . into a liquid by heating and the reverse change can be brought about by cooling.

5. To effect minor . . . of the rate of . . . of the balance wheel, many watches are supplied with a small lever, one arm of which can be moved along a scale on a small metal plate.

6. The gas jar is arranged to collect gas by downward . . . .

7. The spring balance reading will continue to get smaller until the stone is completely immersed, but there will be no change in the reading as the stone is lowered to a greater . . . .

8. The heating of limestone is carried out on a large scale in the . . . of quicklime, which is the name commonly used for the calcium oxide produced.

9. We cannot feel the . . . of the atmosphere pressing on us because our blood exerts an outward . . . equal to the . . . exerted by the air.

10. The . . . of heat in a room in winter is an important point, while in summer it is necessary to keep the house cool.

III GRAMMAR

EXERCISE A *Articles*

Write down the following passage, inserting *a, an* or *the*, where necessary, in the blank spaces.

Although . . . atmosphere exerts . . . very great pressure, we do not feel this pressure weighing down on us. This is because there is . . . blood inside our bodies which exerts . . . same pressure as . . . air outside. We can show . . . pressure which is exerted by . . . atmosphere by means of . . . following experiment. Take . . . tin can which has . . . screw top and put . . . little water in it. Place . . . can on . . . stove and heat it until . . . water boils and . . . steam comes out of . . . open top. . . . steam is . . . water vapour mixed with . . . air, so if . . . steam comes out of . . . can, then . . . air comes out as well. Now remove . . . can from . . . stove and screw . . . cap on . . . top. Allow . . . can to cool, and see what happens. When . . . can is hot, . . . pressure inside it is atmospheric and is due to . . . pressure exerted by . . . steam and . . . air inside . . . can. But as . . . steam inside . . . can cools down and condenses . . . remaining air and . . . water vapour will exert . . . less pressure than . . . air outside because some of . . . air has passed out of . . . can with . . . steam. . . . air outside . . . can now exerts more pressure than . . . air inside it, and this outside pressure will be enough to make . . . can collapse.

EXERCISE B *Prepositions*

Write out the sentences, putting an appropriate preposition in each blank space:
1. The rubber suckers often used . . . fixing hooks . . . shop windows remain . . . place because the air has been squeezed out . . . between the rubber and the glass and the air pressing . . . the outer surface . . . the rubber pushes it firmly . . . the glass.
2. A knowledge . . . magnetic declination is . . . great importance . . . navigation as allowance must be made . . . it . . . finding true directions . . . compass readings.
3. It is usual to say that the positive current flows . . . the circuit . . . the positive . . . the negative terminal, that is, . . . the direction shown . . . the arrows . . . the diagram.
4. To enable one temperature to be compared . . . another, thermometers are marked . . . scales . . . degrees and it is obvious that for comparisons . . . readings taken . . . different thermometers to be made these scales must be marked . . . some stated way.
5. Magnetize a length . . . knitting needle and push it . . . a cork so that it will float upright . . . a trough . . . water . . . its north pole a little . . . the water surface.

6. The actual state . . . a substance, whether solid, liquid or gaseous, . . . a particular time depends . . . its temperature, and a change . . . state . . . one form . . . another can be achieved . . . heating or cooling.

7. A substance . . . iron may have its size altered . . . being moderately heated, but it still remains a piece . . . iron and, apart . . . the change . . . size, its properties are unchanged.

8. Lead accumulators are secondary cells. . . . this we mean that the chemical changes which take place . . . the cell when it is giving ?. . . current can be reversed . . . driving a current . . . it . . . the opposite direction . . . the current it gives . . ., so that it can be brought back . . . its original condition and recharged . . . producing current again.

EXERCISE C *Verb forms*

Put the verb in brackets into its correct form:

Substances (consist of) small parts, or particles, which (know) as molecules. Molecules (compose of) atoms. Some substances, like salt and water for example, (have) molecules which (can, analyse) further into other substances. If a molecule of water (analyse), for example, it (find, consist of) two atoms of hydrogen and one atom of oxygen. Substances whose molecules (compose of) atoms of other substances (know) as compounds. Other substances (have) molecules which (can, break down) into atoms of other substances, and these (call) elements. Hydrogen and oxygen, for example (be) elements. Thus if a molecule of oxygen (analyse) it (find, consist of) only atoms of oxygen and not of any other substance. There (be) 92 natural elements. Some (be) metallic solids like copper, iron and lead; some (be) non-metallic solids like sulphur and carbon; and some (be) gases like oxygen, hydrogen and nitrogen.

IV REPORT WRITING

Study the following columns carefully:

DIRECTIONS ETC.	DESCRIPTION	REPORT
Take a displacement vessel and a measuring jar. Pour water into the vessel until it overflows into the measuring jar. Read the level of the water surface in the measuring jar.	Water is poured into the displacement vessel until it overflows through the pipe into the measuring jar. The level of the water surface in the measuring jar is read, and then the solid is lowered into the vessel	Water was poured into the displacement vessel until it overflowed through the pipe into the measuring jar. The level of the water surface in the measuring jar was read and then the solid was

DIRECTIONS ETC.	DESCRIPTION	REPORT
Lower the solid into the vessel until it is completely covered by the water. Water is displaced and flows down the pipe into the measuring jar. Read the level of the water surface in the measuring jar again. The volume displaced is equal to the volume of the body.	until it is completely covered by the water. Water is displaced and flows down the pipe into the measuring jar, and the level of the water surface in the measuring jar is read again. The volume of water displaced is equal to the volume of the body.	lowered into the vessel until it was completely covered by the water. Water was displaced and flowed down the pipe into the measuring jar, and the level of the water surface in the measuring jar was read again. The volume of water displaced was equal to the volume of the body.

EXERCISE A

Change the descriptions in Exercise D 1, Unit 6 (p. 71) into reports, using the above columns as a guide.

EXERCISE B

Change your answers to Exercise D 2, Unit 6 (p. 72) into reports.

EXERCISE C

Carry out the following experiments, and then write reports of them. Illustrate your reports with diagrams where you think this is necessary.

(i) Fill a drinking glass to the brim with water. Place a piece of cardboard over it. Hold the cardboard against the glass and turn the glass upside down. Take away the hand holding the cardboard. What happens? What does this experiment show about air?

(ii) Remove the brass shell from a used electric bulb by gently heating it in a gas or alcohol flame. When the sealing wax begins to smoke, grasp the shell with a pair of pliers and twist it away from the glass bulb. Observe the end of the sealed tube, extending from the bulb through which the air is removed. Place the bulb, tube end down, in a jar of coloured water. With a pair of pliers, snip the end of the tube (while under water). What happens? How do you explain this?

(iii) Place manganese (IV) oxide powder in a flask and fit a thistle funnel and a delivery tube into the stopper of the flask. Place the end of the delivery tube in a trough containing brine and place a jar containing a column of brine upside down in the trough, supported by a shelf, so that the end of the delivery tube is beneath the open end of the jar. Drop concentrated hydrochloric acid on to the manganese (IV) oxide through the thistle funnel and heat the flask. What happens?

(iv) Magnetize a piece of clock spring or a hacksaw blade about 25 cm long by stroking it with a magnet. Test the magnet you have made with a compass to be sure that it has a north pole at one end and a south pole at the other. Mark the poles N and S with chalk. Does the compass show any polarity at the centre of the magnet? Use a pair of pliers and break the long magnet into two parts each about 12·5 cm long. Test the polarity of each end of the two magnets. What do you observe? Mark the poles of each magnet N and S. Now break the two magnets into four magnets. Test each end and mark them as N and S. Continue dividing the magnets, as many times as you can. What does this experiment suggest?

V   ESSAY WRITING

Write a short essay based on the following notes. Combine the sentences in any way you wish, changing the grammatical patterns if necessary. Divide your essay into paragraphs and give the essay a title.

carbon is present in all organic compounds
it is an essential constituent of all plant and animal cells
it is familiar to us in the form of a black substance
this substance is known as charcoal
charcoal is obtained from wood by heating logs
the logs are heated in a certain way
only a small quantity of the wood burns
charcoal is amorphous
this means that the particles of the solid are not crystalline
coke and soot consist mainly of amorphous carbon
diamond and graphite are forms of carbon
diamond and graphite are crystalline
graphite is used as a lubricant
it is used in the manufacture of 'lead' pencils
it is used in the carbon rods for electric cells
diamond is the hardest substance known
diamond is brilliant
a multitude of reflections of light fall upon the cut stone
diamond is much sought after as jewellery
diamond is hard
it is used for making the tips on industrial cutting tools
graphite and diamond contain identical carbon atoms
the two forms of carbon have marked differences
the two forms are called allotropes
diamond is very strong: how can we explain this?
the atoms of diamond are regularly arranged

each atom is held rigidly in position by four bonds
these bonds link the atom to its four nearest neighbours
in graphite the atoms exist in layers
the layers are only loosely held together
adjacent layers of carbon atoms can slide easily over one another
carbon monoxide, carbon dioxide = the principal oxides of carbon
charcoal will burn in air or oxygen
it forms carbon dioxide
$C+O_2 = CO_2$
carbon combines with oxygen very readily
it is often used as a reducing agent
lead oxide is heated with charcoal
small pellets of lead will be formed
the lead oxide is reduced by the charcoal
$2PbO+C = 2Pb+CO_2$
carbon monoxide may be produced in the laboratory
carbon dioxide is generated in a flask
dilute hydrochloric acid acts on marble (calcium carbonate)
the carbon dioxide is passed through a long hard-glass tube
the tube is filled with red-hot charcoal
the carbon dioxide is reduced
it reacts again with the carbon
it gives off carbon monoxide
the carbon monoxide is collected in a gas jar
$CO_2+C = 2CO$
carbon monoxide must not be allowed to escape into the air
it is extremely poisonous
it is often formed in brightly-glowing coal fires
it is often formed in the coke fires in watchmen's braziers
don't take a brazier fire into a closed shed
this is very dangerous
carbon monoxide burns with a blue flame
it is used industrially
it is used as a fuel in producer gas and water gas
carbon dioxide combines with water
it makes carbonic acid
the carbonates are the salts of carbonic acid
calcium carbonate is an example
most carbonates are insoluble
they yield carbon dioxide
heat them or treat them with acids
heat copper carbonate: $CuCO_3 = CuO+CO_2$
treat with hydrochloric acid: $CuCO_3+2HCl = CuCl_2+CO_2(g)+H_2O$
half fill a large test-tube with lime-water
pass carbon dioxide into it

calcium carbonate is precipitated
this causes cloudiness in the lime-water
continue to pass carbon dioxide into the solution
eventually all the calcium hydroxide will have been precipitated
it forms calcium carbonate
calcium carbonate can now be converted into calcium bicarbonate
more carbon dioxide reacts with the water of the solution
$$CaCO_3 + CO_2 + H_2O = Ca(HCO_3)_2$$
the bicarbonate is soluble in water
the carbonate is insoluble
the bicarbonate dissolves as it is formed
the cloudiness disappears
boil the solution
the extra carbon dioxide is driven out
the bicarbonate is decomposed
calcium carbonate is precipitated
the liquid becomes cloudy again
$$Ca(HCO_3)_2 = CaCO_3(s) + H_2O + CO_2$$